I0791542

Seeking the Common Good through Public Policy

Justice leaders Dr. Martin Luther King, Jr., Dorothy Day, Dietrich Bonhoeffer, and Harriet Tubman portrayed at Luther Place Memorial Church in Washington D.C.

GARY E. MARING

Lulu Publishing Services rev. date: 03/09/2021

Seeking the Common Good through Public Policy

With a case study on ending long-term homelessness in the nation's capital

Gary E. Maring, February 2021

In this book, Gary Maring shares a vital message for our times and a compelling vision for our "common good." Maring offers us an informed and realistic perspective on social justice which is inclusive of all persons and accountable to our history. As one of the founders of the N Street Village (NSV) programs nearly 50 years ago, Gary has a long history of advocating for and helping found programs serving those who are impoverished or homeless. He has served many years on the Board of NSV and in recent years on the DC Ineragency Council on Homelessness' Strategic Planning Committee. In this book, he provides a special focus on efforts to end long term homelessness in Washington DC and the role of NSV in addressing the particular challenges of women who are homeless here in our nation's capital. Maring's personal work and experience combine herein with his considerable intellect and rigorous research to offer readers a meaningful moral compass and a practical policy pathway pointing us all toward true "common good."

Schroeder Stribling
CEO, N Street Village
http://www.nstreetvillage.org

Gary Maring, is a part of the congregation I serve in DC, Luther Place Church, where for over 50 years, he has been a congregational leader and a social justice advocate. In this book, Gary discusses the important concept of the 'common good' where all members of the community receive sustenance and human dignity. The common good is central to the tenets of many religious faiths and remains imperative in our challenging times of COVID-19 where so many are suffering. Gary has been instrumental in helping found several key social justice programs at Luther Place over the decade — N Street Village, now DC's largest program for homeless women, the national Lutheran Volunteer Corps, and the Steinbruck Center. Additionally, over the long term, Gary been engaged in community organizing through interfaith justice coalitions in the DC area. Gary regularly organizes with the Washington Interfaith Network with its focus on housing and jobs, the Congregation Action Network which advocates on immigration policy and he participates in the Poor People's Campaign which continues the economic justice work started by Martin Luther King, Jr. some 57 years ago. We are grateful for the ways Gary bears witness to his faith and the common good in public life!

Pastor Karen Brau
Luther Place Memorial Church
Washington, DC

About the Author

Gary Maring is a member of Luther Place Memorial Church, a progressive Lutheran church in Washington, DC, only blocks from the White House, which has served the nation's capital for nearly 150 years. He is among the key founders and a board member of N Street Village, a continuum of programs and supportive housing for women who are (or have) experiencing homelessness in DC, and he serves on the DC Interagency Council on Homelessness' Strategic Planning Committee. Mr. Maring is also a founder of the national Lutheran Volunteer Corps, which places yearlong volunteers in social justice agencies in DC and multiple cities around the United States. He is also among the founders of the Steinbruck Center at Luther Place Church which hosts groups participating in experiences related to justice, education, service, and community engagement including college alternative breaks, protests and activism, conferences, and more. He has been a longtime advocate for social justice and the common good in the public policy arena. He writes a regular blog on social justice and public policy, which can be viewed at http://gary-maring.blogspot.com. He is president of Maring Publishing: The Common Good and Public Policy, LLC, in Maryland, the entity under which he publishes blogs, books, and articles. His professional career was in transportation policy in the federal government, which helps him understand the challenges of formulating national policy and legislation that he discusses in his book with regard to justice issues.

Acknowledgments and Dedication

I dedicate this book to my dear wife Margaret and to our beloved children and grandchildren. I also want to offer special acknowledgment to the remarkable pastors of Luther Place Memorial church in DC who so influenced my life over more than fifty years, i.e., Jim Singer, John Steinbruck, Bob Holum, and my current pastor Karen Brau. They taught me the key justice messages of the gospel. Two important gospel messages that particularly inspired our justice work at Luther Place were 'welcoming the stranger' and caring for the disenfranchised or 'least of these'. Finally, I want to pay tribute in memoriam to my longtime friends and mentors, Dale McDaniel and Chuck Solem, who served tirelessly over many decades to support justice work at Luther Place church and N Street Village programs for homeless women.

Contents

Preface

I am increasingly drawn to the concept of the **common good**, which to me means a society where everyone has access to the basic necessities of life—a place to live, food to eat, and access to education, employment, health care, and human dignity. The concept of the common good is central to the tenets of many religious faiths and closely related to the principle of the Golden Rule, i.e., doing unto others as we would wish done unto ourselves. Seeking the common good implies that all members of a society should have reasonable access to its benefits and enjoyment. Our country embeds this concept in the Declaration of Independence: "We hold these truths to be self-evident, that all men are created equal, that they are endowed by their Creator with certain unalienable Rights, that among these are Life, Liberty, and the pursuit of Happiness."

I generally apply a few simple tests to help discern whether our leaders and their policies are just and supportive of the common good:

1. Are our elected leaders and their policies supportive of the needs of all segments of society?
2. Are our elected leaders and their policies acting in the interests of my children's and grandchildren's future?
3. Do the leaders and their policies support the biblical concepts of compassion for the disenfranchised and the Golden Rule, which is common to most all faith traditions?

In my previous book, *Faith, Social Justice, and Public Policy: A Progressive's View,* I explored the interrelationships between faith and social justice and how those concepts relate to public policy.[1] In this book, I go deeper into these concepts, particularly the theme of the common good and how it affects local and national public policies. I discuss methods that have been and are being used to translate these concepts into policy that is more just for all of society's members.

Although major human rights movements have brought significant economic and social gains in recent decades for women, people of color, and sexual minorities, those victories also carried with them a backlash. Such pushback is seen particularly from some in the white working-class, who, while having some legitimate economic grievances, unfortunately tend to blame the rise of minorities, immigrants, and women for their diminished economic status. The "Let's Make America Great Again" political campaign theme in 2016 and 2020 implied restoring predominant white male privilege of decades ago and diminishing upward mobility for minorities and women. Of course, no politician will be able to restore the old economic order given our twenty-first-century global economy, ongoing technological innovation, and the hard-won civil rights and workplace antidiscrimination laws that are now in place.

At this time in our history, more than ever in my lifetime, I believe we are called to stand up to forces trying to roll back decades of social justice accomplishments in areas such as civil rights, health care, voting rights, racial justice, gender equity, income equality, environmental justice, immigration, and the like. When minority groups are publicly denigrated by our leaders and made to feel fear for their families, then we must resist. We can learn from past and current human rights movements like abolition, women's suffrage, civil rights, freedom to marry, #MeToo, Black Lives Matter, and others. I had planned to release my book in the spring of 2020 but paused as the pandemics of COVID-19 and racial injustice quickly emerged through the year. Just before my book publication, the country witnessed the election of a woman of color as Vice President of the United States, a truly historic event that gives hope to many in our society who have been disenfranchised. I have attempted to capture the profound events and common good lessons from this tumultuous period in our history and offer some modest insights regarding our path forward knowing the journey will be long.

On a mural on a door of our church Luther Place in DC as pictured on the cover, Dr. Martin Luther King, Jr. reminds us that we must walk together and always march ahead; and as he frequently cited from a portion of a sermon delivered in 1853 by the abolitionist minister Theodore Parker, "The arc of the moral universe is long, but it bends toward justice."

Introduction

During the last century, America has seen unparalleled improvement in our economic and social conditions, but much remains to be done. The Industrial Revolution was emerging in the late nineteenth century, but market forces were also causing significant negative social conditions in what was often referred to as the Gilded Age. This helped spur a period of social activism and reform, resulting in major social justice accomplishments in the first half of the twentieth century such as workplace regulations (e.g., child labor laws), fair wages, women's suffrage, government reform and civil service, social security and unemployment measures, industrial reform and regulation, environmental conservation, and more.

President Theodore Roosevelt (1901–09) challenged the Gilded Age inequities and was a key champion of the environmental conservation movement. Roosevelt developed a philosophy that became known as the Square Deal, which expanded the government's regulatory powers to curb excesses that had emerged in the marketplace but also championed government reform to improve its effectiveness. The forces set in motion by Theodore Roosevelt were further built upon by subsequent presidents, in particular, his cousin Franklin Delano Roosevelt, whose New Deal then led to unparalleled economic growth and social well-being in the post–World War II period. This was followed by the Great Society, a set of domestic programs launched by President Johnson in the mid-1960s spurred by the Civil Rights movement. Key goals of Johnson's efforts included addressing poverty and racial injustice. New major spending programs that addressed education, medical care, urban problems, rural poverty, and transportation were launched during this period, and the Civil Rights and Voting Rights Acts in 1964–1965 addressed racial disparities. Medicare and Medicaid were enacted during this period also. When environmental concerns emerged because of unprecedented post–World War II industrial growth and greatly increased automobile travel, environmental activism and legislation emerged, including the 1963 Clean Air Act, the 1972 Clean Water Act, and the 1974 Safe Drinking Water Act, along with creation of the US Environmental Protection Agency (EPA). These initiatives drew broad bipartisan support.

Unfortunately, in recent years we have seen pushback against some of these policies and have witnessed growing economic inequality, racial tensions, anti-immigrant sentiments, and political polarization. We see economic and social distress in many Rust Belt communities due in part to loss of manufacturing and extractive industry jobs caused by technology and globalization. Further, our country's demographics are changing, and this is unsettling to many whites, particularly in more rural states and communities. Both the economic and the social unrest drove many in these communities to vote for what they saw as a candidate who would bring change in the 2016 presidential election. Unfortunately, the resulting change has too often been counter to the common good as will be discussed herein. Now, as we enter 2021, the nation witnessed an important political transition with incoming President Joe Biden and Vice President Kamala Harris. The last days of the Trump administration, including the white supremacist assault on the Capitol, was one of the worst periods in American history and will leave an indelible stain on our democracy. So many immediate challenges face the new Biden administration, most notably COVID-19 and related health care and economic displacement issues. They have many proposals for new health, economic, racial equity, immigration, environmental policies and importantly bringing a deeply divided country together. This will all be a huge challenge, but the Biden administration has assembled a very experienced and diverse Cabinet and now with control of Congress they hope to move aggressively to implement needed change.

The COVID-19 pandemic painfully reminded us of the deep inequities in our society and the need to find common ground in addressing our emerging economic, social, and environmental challenges. Kay Coles James, founder and board chair of The Gloucester Institute and president of the Heritage Foundation recently commented that, "We are all in the same storm but not all in the same boat…Some are in yachts, some are in rowboats, and some are barely staying alive with a life jacket." The COVID-19 crisis laid bare the systemic inequities and structural racism that many persons and communities experience daily. Many hope that the twin pandemics of 2020 will lead to new policies and legislation addressing continuing racial and economic disparities in our nation.

This book is focused on a simple but particularly important concept, **the common good**, which I discuss further in the next chapter. A deeply related moral principle is even more familiar to us—the Golden Rule, to "do unto others as you would have them do unto you." In national surveys, nearly 90 percent of the US population say that they believe in the Golden Rule as an important guiding principle in their lives, yet we are in one of the most polarized periods in my lifetime. We too often see hate language pervading our public dialogue. We see anti-minority, anti-immigrant, anti-Semitic, anti-gay, and racist attitudes too often entering our public discourse. At the same time, we still witness great inequalities in our social order worsened by the COVID-19 pandemic.

Following are some, but not all, of the key social and economic justice issues of the day that are significant detractors to achieving the common good in America.

Economic inequality—Economic inequality has received increased attention in recent decades. In September 2019, the Census Bureau reported that in 2018 income inequality in the United States had hit its highest level since the bureau started tracking it more than five decades ago.[2] Census data showed that in 2018, more than half (53 percent) of all money income went to the wealthiest fifth of the population. And in 2020, the sudden emergence of the coronavirus further devastated low- and moderate-income workers in particular. A disproportionate number of minorities are front line workers, and this factor has been a significant contributor to the much higher COVID-19 infection and death rates among Blacks and Latinos.

Poverty and homelessness—The US poverty rate declined modestly in the last few years before COVID-19, but in 2019 it was only slightly below the level of 2007, right before the Great Recession pushed millions of Americans out of work and into financial distress. About 34 million Americans lived in poverty in 2019 and it was more prevalent among African Americans and Hispanics. Then in 2020 our nation suffered another recession due to COVID-19 and millions more have likely been pushed into poverty. Recent research on the impact of living in poor neighborhoods shows that the negative effects extend across generations, which demonstrates that neighborhood inequality that exists in one generation is commonly transmitted to the next. This and other factors causing intergenerational poverty and persistent disadvantage impede individuals' ability to achieve the American dream. Recent analysis by the National Low-Income Housing Coalition has found that a full-time worker earning the federal minimum wage of $7.25 per hour cannot rent an affordable (30 percent of one's income) two-bedroom apartment anywhere in the country.[3] Further, such low-income individuals and families living on the margins are vulnerable to unexpected crises like COVID-19, which can leave them destitute and possibly homeless.

Racial justice—In recent years, the nation has seen a surge in white nationalism, voting restrictions, and gerrymandering that often disadvantage African Americans and other minorities, and increased racially motivated violence. In 2020, we have sadly witnessed the disproportionate impact of the coronavirus pandemic on minorities followed by multiple high-profile police killings of African Americans which resulted in nationwide protests led by Black Lives Matter (BLM). Major pressure has built for police reform, but more broadly to address systemic racism in America. In recent decades, mass incarceration has disproportionately taken Black men out of the job market, disqualified them from benefits such as food stamps, increased their risk of homelessness, and increased their chances of reincarceration. And with this high rate of imprisonment of Black men, already vulnerable Black families and the women who sustain them have been plummeted into greater poverty and stress when their loved ones are incarcerated.

Gender and family issues—Work–life balance is a top workplace concern for women in America, followed by family leave, childcare issues, and pay equity. Both men and women work more hours than in other developed countries with fewer family benefits (such as sick/family leave and childcare). The lack of these benefits has been vividly revealed during the coronavirus outbreak. Sexual harassment has emerged as a national concern, and we have witnessed a broad social media movement known as #MeToo as part of an awareness campaign to illustrate the pervasive sexual abuse and harassment that women have experienced and still experience. The pandemic has further laid bare the lack of family leave benefits and the challenges of childcare with the heaviest burden falling on women.

Gay rights—The 2015 Supreme Court decision supporting marriage equality was a milestone accomplishment after advocates had built the case through many legal challenges at the state and local levels over the previous decade and more. This has resulted in pushback from some religious groups that want religious exemptions that would effectively allow discrimination based on sexual orientation. Importantly, in June 2020, the Supreme Court ruled that the 1964 civil rights law protects gay and transgender workers from workplace discrimination.

Immigration—The recent anti-immigrant trends are certainly not the first emergence of nativism in the United States against immigrants. Back during the founding years of the Republican Party, Abraham Lincoln strongly challenged the nativism coming from the likes of the "Know-Nothing Party." Similar sentiments emerged in the early twentieth century under President Wilson. In recent years, we have again seen pushback on immigration at a time when we need immigrants to help build a future workforce; the natural birth rate in the US and in European countries is not high enough to produce a sufficient future workforce. Clearly, our immigration system needs reform, but building walls on the borders to keep immigrants out is not the answer, although it paid politically to certain base instincts.

Health care—The Affordable Care Act (ACA), enacted in 2010 with President Obama's leadership, has reduced the number of uninsured people by more than 20 million, and it has concurrently increased access to primary care, needed surgeries, medicines, and treatment for chronic conditions. As a result, according to studies conducted at Harvard University, the ACA is saving tens of thousands of lives each year. Unfortunately, the Trump administration and Republicans in Congress persistently attempted to undo this long-sought expansion of health coverage without any plan for what would replace it. Despite the success of the ACA, nearly 30 million Americans are still without health coverage, and costs are higher than in other, comparable countries. With the coronavirus pandemic having caused more than 500,000 American deaths, health care has emerged as a priority issue for the country and has highlighted the importance of quickly moving to universal health care. Instead, the Trump Administration and Republican state attorneys general brought yet another ACA repeal case before the Supreme Court for hearing in late 2020. This was truly an insane policy in the midst of a catastrophic health crisis.

Voting rights—Here in the twenty-first century, we have inherited the broad voting rights that came about only after a long struggle. It took nearly two centuries for the nation to move toward a model approaching universal suffrage. But as far as we have come, we see states still trying to enact voter restrictions, many of which disproportionately affect minority groups. The right to vote is a fundamental right in our country that has been hard-earned, and we should be making extraordinary efforts to get everyone out to vote rather than implementing backdoor and discriminatory schemes to limit voters' opportunity to exercise their constitutional right. With the coronavirus pandemic, voting has become much more challenging, and the vast majority of states wisely allowed expanded vote by mail options for the 2020 elections. Still, we saw one political party and its leader try innumerable schemes to suppress and challenge the vote before and after the 2020 Presidential election; truly shameful after centuries of struggle for the precious right to vote.

Environmental sustainability—Reflecting upon and celebrating together the substantial bipartisan environmental accomplishments of recent decades, with due credit to the Republican presidents who signed most of the historic environmental acts, we desperately need to form some bipartisan consensus again. Unfortunately, President Trump removed the United States from the Paris climate agreement and rolled back many climate related regulations but with the Biden Presidency we are seeing a rapid reversal as climate change increasingly looms as a primary environmental threat. We recently learned that the year 2020 tied with 2016 as the warmest years on record. We currently witness more rapid glacier melting, more frequent severe weather events, and massive fires. Irreversible climate-induced catastrophes are likely in this century and beyond if action is not taken to slow carbon emissions.

Unless we come together and solve these multifaceted social, economic, and environmental problems, whose solutions are in our mutual interest, the nation's economy, social cohesion, and environmental sustainability will inevitably decline. With the seeming loss of capacity for meaningful national dialogue and lack of agreement on basic facts and scientific hypotheses (such as climate change), finding ways to take meaningful action becomes increasingly difficult. Our politicians seem only to inflame the divisions rather than to seek the common good. If we are unable to address these problems, our children and grandchildren will be the ones to suffer; is that what we want as our legacy? The new Biden Administration is beginning the long process of healing our nation and we are all challenged to help in that much needed effort.

1

Social Justice and the Common Good

The common good and social justice are interrelated concepts; to live in a good society is to live in a just society, and if we are to live in a just society, our economic life and institutions must be oriented to policies that are beneficial to society as a whole. Elements of the common good include but are not limited to food, health, education, shelter, energy, environmental stewardship, transportation, peace, security, freedom, and human dignity. Social justice is present when people enjoy universal access to common good elements.

As noted in the preface, the concept of the common good is central to the tenets of many religious faiths and can be succinctly described as doing unto others as we would wish done unto ourselves (i.e., the Golden Rule). Historians suggest that Aristotle was the first to articulate an ethical understanding of the common good, followed by Augustine and Thomas Aquinas, who developed the concept into standard moral theology. The common good became a central concept in Catholic social teaching. According to the Vatican II Gaudium et Spes in 1965, "it is imperative that no one … indulge in a merely individualistic morality. The best way to fulfill one's obligations of justice and love is to

> **Social justice** is present when people enjoy universal access to **common good elements** such as food, shelter, health care, and education.

contribute to the common good according to one's means and the needs of others, and also to promote and help public and private organizations devoted to bettering the conditions of life."

Many religious traditions and humanist organizations embrace tenets of compassion and the common good. Karen Armstrong, religious historian and author of the book *History of God* and many other interreligious publications, has identified compassion as the most important tenet among the world's major religions, suggesting it is indispensable to the creation of a just economy and a peaceful global community. Building on this belief, she initiated the Charter for Compassion in 2009 to promote the principles of the Golden Rule across the religious and global spectrum. The charter was unveiled by Karen Armstrong and the Council of Conscience on November 12, 2009, at the National Press Club in Washington, DC.

The charter affirms the following:

- Compassion is celebrated in all major religious, spiritual, and ethical traditions.
- The Golden Rule is our prime duty and cannot be limited to our own political, religious, or ethnic group.
- Therefore, in our divided world, compassion can build common ground.

Both the Old and New Testaments of the Bible contain many references to the concepts of the common good and justice. For example:

- "He has told you, mortal one, what is good; And what does the LORD require of you But to do justice, to love kindness, And to walk humbly with your God?" (Micah 6:8).

- "Always seek after that which is good for one another and for all people" (1 Thessalonians 5:15).
- "Seek the welfare (shalom) of the city where I have sent you into exile and pray to the LORD on its behalf; for in its welfare you will have welfare" (Jeremiah 29:7).

Among our country's founders, James Madison wrote in *The Federalist Papers* of the "public," "common," or "general" good as closely tied with justice and declared that justice is the desired end of government and civil society. And of course, Thomas Jefferson wrote in the Declaration of Independence, "We hold these truths to be self-evident, that all men are created equal."

I believe that only when we as a nation have more concern for the common good than for rugged individualism can we truly consider ourselves exceptional. Bill Ivey, in his book *Handmaking America: A Back-to-Basics Pathway to a Revitalized American Democracy*, articulates the concept as follows: "America must be a nation in which every citizen can live with purpose through work, family, and community; where the elderly, helpless, and fearful are not alone; a society that stands proudly to the world as a beacon on the hill."

Columnist David Brooks comments that individual rights have become dominant in America, but the roots of common obligation seem to be withering away. He says that freedom is important, but without a unifying national purpose, we too often see polarization and political war. Columnist Robert J. Samuelson once wrote about society's choice between one where people accept modest sacrifices for a common good or one where groups selfishly protect their own interests.

Professor Michael Sandel of Harvard University advocates a "politics of the common good." In a series of lectures delivered at Georgetown University in 2009, Sandel challenged a strictly market-based public policy. He called for a move back to politics that also considers moral and religious values—that is, considerations of the common good. For example, he believes health care should not be strictly a market consideration; most developed countries consider it a moral imperative to provide access to health care for everyone. He also highlights that the inequality in incomes is the worst since World War II. This is destructive of the common good and leads to extreme gaps between the privileged and the common person.

Disagreements are bound to sometimes undercut the nation's ability to evoke a sustained and widespread commitment to the common good. With our great diversity, efforts to bring about the common good can sometimes lead to adopting or promoting the views of some while excluding others, violating the principle of treating people equally. Resolving those trade-offs in the political arena is the great challenge of our democracy.

Pope Francis addressed some of the United States' thorniest political issues during his historic visit to the US in 2015 by urging the world's wealthiest nation to welcome immigrants, address poverty, end homelessness, and do more to address climate change. Pope Francis invoked the term "common good" several times in his address to Congress, including when he remarked, "Politics is … an expression of our compelling need to live as one, in order to build as one, the greatest 'common good' … A political society endures when it seeks, as a vocation, to satisfy common needs by stimulating the growth of all its members, especially those in situations of greater vulnerability or risk."

The vision of a "beloved community" captures the essence of the common good. The term "beloved community" can be traced back to Josiah Royce, the nineteenth-century American religious philosopher. Royce characterized the beloved community as "a spiritual or divine community capable of achieving the highest good as well as the common good." Dr. Martin Luther King Jr. popularized the idea of the beloved community as a society based on justice, equal opportunity, and love of one's fellow human beings. Dr. King in his final Christmas Eve sermon in 1967 highlighted that we are all tied in a common destiny, and whatever affects one affects all.

Walter Brueggemann observes in his book *Journey to the Common Good*, "We face a crisis about the common good [today] because there are powerful forces at work among us to resist the common good, to violate community solidarity, and to deny a common destiny. Mature people, at their best, are committed to the common good that reaches beyond private interest, transcends sectarian commitments, and offers human solidarity." Louis Cozolino of Pepperdine University wisely says, "We are not the survival of the fittest, we are the survival of the nurtured." We must find ways to increasingly widen the circle of compassion in our country and world.

The American Academy of Arts and Sciences released an important report on this topic in June 2020 entitled, *Our Common Purpose: Reinventing American Democracy for the 21st Century*. The report of the Academy's Commission on the Practice of Democratic Citizenship offers a broad set of recommendations around equality of voice and representation, empowering voters, and inspiring a culture of commitment to American constitutional democracy focused on the common good.

Vote Common Good is a relatively new interfaith nonprofit in the US committed to encouraging voting for the common good rather than for strictly what is best for the individual, a political party, or a particular institution. It states that "good-hearted Christians, Jews, Muslims, and people of all traditions cannot simply vote for what is best for themselves as individuals or even what is best for their religion, party, race, or nation alone, but must be concerned for the common good. Or to put it differently, selfish people of every religion and tradition vote for self-interest or partisan interest alone, but good people of every religion vote for the common good."

On October 19, 2007, the Dalai Lama visited the programs for homeless women at N Street Village (NSV) in Washington, DC (note: I will elaborate on NSV in subsequent chapters), and I was privileged to greet him and hear him speak. At that event, he stressed compassion for "the least of these" as he embraced the homeless women of NSV (see accompanying photo); he said that compassion and social justice are the common messages of all the world's major religions. While lamenting that the twentieth century was a century of bloodshed, with two world wars, the Holocaust, wars in Korea and Vietnam, and genocides in Armenia, Cambodia, Bosnia, and Rwanda, among other conflicts around the globe, he said that he remained hopeful for the future… Despite its faltering start, the twenty-first century could become a great opportunity for dialogue, one in which compassion and the seeds of nonviolence will be able to flourish." He also emphasized, "Climate change in particular is a challenge that calls us more than ever to make a common effort to defend the common good."

The Dalai Lama at N Street Village in DC, 2007

2

Religion, Social Justice, and the Common Good

My previous book focused on the intersection of faith, social justice, and public policy and the biblical underpinnings to concepts of compassion and justice for all in society. This book builds on that understanding and goes deeper into the concept of the common good and implications for public policy.

Robert Jones of the Public Religion Research Institute (PRRI) writes in his book *Progressive and Religious* that the heart of the religious life should be not only personal piety but also addressing structural injustice.[4] Unfortunately, the face of Christianity in America today is often not about compassion and justice; rather, as theologian Brian McLaren, author of *a New Kind of Christianity,* says that many churches have aligned themselves with American nationalism and partisanism and that he thinks is dangerous. Ever since the so-called Christian Moral Majority (often referred to as the religious right or evangelicals) emerged in support of Ronald Reagan's presidency in the 1980s, they have been counted on to largely support the Republican presidential candidate, principally because of cultural issues such as abortion and gay rights. And disturbingly to many of faith, evangelicals went overwhelmingly for Donald Trump in 2016 and 2020 even though Russell Moore, president of the Ethics and Religious Liberty Commission of the Southern

Baptist Convention, said in a 2016 *New York Times* op-ed that evangelical Christians would have to "repudiate everything they believe" to support Trump.

In his 2017 book *The End of White Christian America,* Robert Jones explains and analyzes the various forces that are contributing to the decline of white Christian America. He says, "Attitudes on key cultural issues like gay marriage—an issue that was really at the heart of conservative Christian politics—have changed dramatically. Whenever you have that kind of rapid change, it does create a sense of vertigo and a sense of worry and anxiety among people." Despite broader acceptance of the LGBTQ community among the American public, the so-called religious right organizations went all out in opposition to same-sex marriage, as illustrated by Focus on the Family head James Dobson, who once wrote to his supporters that the fight against gay marriage would be "our D-Day, or Gettysburg or Stalingrad." But the effort backfired and lost support even among evangelicals. According to PRRI, the fastest positive change on the marriage equality issue occurred among younger evangelicals in recent years. While younger evangelicals are rejecting the extreme views of many of their elders on cultural issues, they are also recognizing that the Christian message is much more about justice than the narrow agenda of their leaders indicates.

Sarah Posner's recent book entitled, *Unholy: Why White Evangelicals Worship at the Altar of Donald Trump*, is an extremely revealing history of the religious right, and its love affair with Donald Trump. She says that the evangelical support for Trump "requires an affirmative buy-in to his alternative reality, where facts are fake news, the press is the enemy of the people, Democratic lawmakers are traitors, and only devout Christians know the real 'truth'." She goes on to say, "Trump's loyal followers see their divine leader as a victim beset by enemies from multiple directions and see themselves as spiritual warriors called by God to protect him…For Trump's evangelical supporters, defending him became indistinguishable from defending White Christian America."

In his new book, *White Too Long: The Legacy of White Supremacy in American Christianity*, Robert Jones reviews the unholy relationship between American Christianity and white supremacy and issues an urgent call for white Christians to reckon with this legacy for the sake of themselves and the nation. As the nation grapples with demographic changes and the legacy of racism, Jones suggests that Christianity's role as a cornerstone of white supremacy has not received much scrutiny. Christians have not just been complicit; rather, as a dominant cultural power in the history of America, they enabled and sustained white supremacy and opposed Black equality over centuries according to Jones. My own family's white Christian history of settlement in Pennsylvania includes displacement of Native Americans and the practice of slavery and that is something our family is still reckoning with.

Liberty University's former president Jerry Falwell Jr., who was an early Trump supporter, called Trump a "dream" president for white evangelicals, and they were the target audience for a film produced by Liberty University and its cinematics department. The film was based on Mark Taylor's 2017 book *The Trump Prophecies*. In the book, Taylor recounts his traumatic experiences as a firefighter and how, suffering from anxiety and depression, he began to hear from both God and evil spirits. He says that God told him that Trump would win the presidential election in 2016. Liberty's cinematics department director, Stephan Schultze, is quoted as telling the Christian Post, "I hope it reflects an understanding that when people come together in prayer, how valuable that is not only for the people that are praying but for what they are praying for ... they have come together in the recognition that those prayers have value and build community and build a strong bond that allows for a president like Donald Trump to be elected. It created a bond within the Christian community." Billy Graham's son Franklin said in 2016 that Trump was "chosen by God." Many evangelical leaders expressed the same, seeing Trump as a "vessel" of God.

> Our first US president, George Washington, set the standard for a leader when he said, "A good moral character is the first essential in a man ... It is therefore highly important that you should endeavor not only to be learned but virtuous." And President Thomas Jefferson added, "God grant that men of principle be our principal men."

Angela Denker, author of *Red State Christians: Understanding the Voters Who Elected Donald Trump*, says we are seeing an increasing religious nationalism that has been strengthened by one of the unlikeliest of alliances. She sees religious nationalism wrapping together the flag, the military, guns, patriotism, and American exceptionalism. She cited a megachurch service that began with the Pledge of Allegiance, the national anthem, and words about honoring our nation's military members—a version of Christianity that wraps together religion, national power, and conservative politics. We already know the dangers of such alliances from Nazi Germany; theologian Dietrich Bonhoeffer gave his life in resistance to a church that had sold its soul to an evil nationalist ideology. A Protestant movement identified as "German Christians" embraced many of the nationalistic and racial aspects of Nazi ideology and supported a "nazified" version of Christianity. The Roman Catholic Church in Germany, supported by the Vatican, signed an accord with the Nazis in 1933 requiring bishops to take an oath of loyalty to the president of the German Reich. History tragically shows us the result of such religious nationalism.

Evangelical Christian author Ben Howe says in his recent book, *The Immoral Majority*, that older white Christians roused to Trump's toxicity because he was seen as taking their side, and they seemed to love his bullying and attacks against his and their enemies. He says that evangelicals "set aside their religiosity and their moral high ground in favor of winning elections, exacting vengeance, and protecting the culture as they saw it." In contrast, it was heartening to see a 2019 editorial in *Christianity Today*, a publication founded by Franklin Graham's father Billy Graham, calling on evangelicals to challenge Trump's immoral behavior, saying, "We are playing with a stacked deck of gross immorality and ethical incompetence … It will crash down on the reputation of evangelical religion and on the world's understanding of the gospel … If we do not reverse course now, will anyone take anything we say about justice and righteousness with any seriousness for decades to come?"[5] A relatively new Christian group called Christians Against Christian Nationalism recently issued a statement of resistance. It says in part,

> Christian nationalism seeks to merge Christian and American identities, distorting both the Christian faith and America's constitutional democracy. Christian nationalism demands Christianity be privileged by the State and implies that to be a good American, one must be Christian. It often overlaps with and provides cover for white supremacy and racial subjugation. We reject this damaging political ideology and invite our Christian brothers and sisters to join

us in opposing this threat to our faith and to our nation … Whether we worship at a church, mosque, synagogue, or temple, America has no second-class faiths. All are equal under the U.S. Constitution.

At the National Prayer Breakfast in February 2020, Arthur Brooks, a Harvard professor and prominent conservative thinker, delivered a passionate plea to Americans to put aside hatred in national life and "love your enemies." Mr. Brooks asked the audience, "How many of you love somebody with whom you disagree politically?" Hands around the room shot up. "I'm going to round that off to 100 percent," he said. But what he did not seem to notice was that President Trump was among those who did not raise his hand. Brooks went on to say, "Contempt is ripping our country apart … We're like a couple on the rocks in this country." And finally, Mr. Brooks added, "Ask God to take political contempt from your heart. And sometimes when it is too hard, ask God to help you fake it." Trump made no effort to fake it when he spoke after Brooks. He proceeded to attack his opponents like Nancy Pelosi and Mitt Romney over the impeachment proceedings, including questioning their faith. This was a shameful moral display by a president at the National Prayer Breakfast, which is intended to bring bipartisan leaders together in peace, reflection, and humility.

My own opinion is that white Christian evangelicals and much of the Republican Party cast their lot with a vision for America that is not consistent with our core democratic values and our multicultural heritage and that is certainly not where I see younger Americans' view of the future heading. For too many, moral leadership was sacrificed for short term political gains.

Unfortunately, US adults see moral leadership as a less important trait for the president than they did roughly two decades ago, a 2018 Gallup poll found.[6] Sixty-six percent said it is an important responsibility of the president, compared to 72 percent who gave that response in polls during the Clinton presidency. Republicans showed the biggest drop in how much they value moral leadership from the president, from 86 percent then to just 63 percent recently. According to a 2018 Quinnipiac University Poll, 90 percent of voters say the president should be a positive influence on children, but only 29 percent said Trump is, while 67 percent said he was not.[7] The majority of voters across nearly every category—gender, education, age, and racial group—deemed Trump a bad role model for children. The one notable exception, the poll found, were Republicans. Seven out of ten Republicans, 72 percent, said Trump was a good influence on children! And I must assume that white evangelicals took much the same view as the Republican Party. During Clinton's impeachment, Jerry Falwell Sr. and many other so-called Moral Majority leaders called for President Clinton's removal because of his moral failings. Many wonder where were the voices of evangelical outrage over President Trump's moral behavior?

A wider split in Christianity is clearly happening. The presiding bishop of the Episcopal Church, Michael Curry, who gave the rousing sermon at the royal wedding of Prince Harry and Meghan Markle in 2018, and other Christian leaders, including progressive evangelical leader Jim Wallis of Sojourners, are leading an alternative mainline Christian movement called Reclaiming Jesus: A Confession of Faith in a Time of Crisis, which has developed a manifesto that says in part, "In this moment of political, moral, and theological crisis in America we are deeply concerned about the resurgence of white nationalism, racism, and xenophobia; misogyny; attacks on immigrants, refugees, and the poor; the regular purveying of falsehoods and consistent lying by the nation's highest leaders; and moves toward autocratic political leadership and authoritarian rule." Now with the transition to a more centrist and inclusive administration led by a person of deep faith commitment, it will be interesting to see how conservative white Christianity responds. The Biden campaign website said, "He will... restore a national culture of inclusiveness that encourages individuals of all faiths to celebrate their beliefs openly and without fear of harm or reprisal."

Friar Richard Rohr who has been inspired by liberation theologian Paulo Freire's work among the poor in Latin America says, "Sadly, there seem to be many Christians who don't even have basic compassion for the poor. In the United States, we are pretty much trained to blame people who are poor, immigrants or refugees, victims, or gay, lesbian, or transgendered people. Far too many seem to think... that if 'those people' would simply work a little more, do things the right way, change their minds, stay hidden, or just 'pray a little harder,' we'd all be better off." He goes on to say, "Our hearts must be softened, and we must experience basic sympathy, empathy, and recognition of another person's pain." My church, Luther Place in DC, pictured in the accompanying image, is part of the Evangelical Lutheran Church of America (ELCA), which views its Christian evangelical heritage quite differently than the evangelical movement of today. We at Luther Place focus on the justice message of the gospel and have devoted ourselves for many years to justice for all, including providing shelter and permanent housing for homeless women through N Street Village (NSV).

Luther Place Memorial Church in DC led by Pastor Karen Brau

Pastor Karen Brau, Luther Place Memorial Church, says,

"We need to pursue three things in this difficult period of history:

- Compassion,
- Community, and
- Calling out evil.

Coming together in community, with compassion for all, gives us the base for confronting evil that is blatant and subtle, loudly and quietly making moves around us today."

Luther Place embraces the biblical concept of "hospitality," that of welcoming the stranger into our midst. Luther Place chose the following biblical texts to be permanently inscribed on the entrance to the facilities for homeless and moderate-income individuals and families at NSV. They capture the essence of the Abrahamic religions' tradition of welcoming the stranger and showing compassion for the disenfranchised or 'least of these':

- "I was a stranger and you welcomed me ... anything you did for the humblest, you did for me" (Matthew 25:35, 40).
- "The stranger who sojourns in your land shall be treated as the native among you" (Leviticus 19:34).

- "Do not neglect to show hospitality to the stranger; for thereby some have entertained angels unawares" (Hebrews 13:2).

Pastor John Steinbruck, who was my pastor and mentor at Luther Place for twenty-seven years, from 1970 to 1997, reflected in numerous writings on welcoming the stranger:

Pastor John Steinbruck served at Luther Place Memorial Church in DC from 1970 to 1997

During that bitter cold winter of 1976, numbers of homeless were freezing and dying of hypothermia. Together with the Community for Creative Non-Violence (CCNV) and Sojourners, more than a thousand letters were sent asking other churches to join in opening their doors to the homeless. Not one response! Jesus said, "Come unto me all ye that labor and are heavy laden. Here in Luther Place you will be welcome to rest." What does that say about the church that has been mandated to welcome the stranger? This is a shared value of all the monotheisms: Christianity, Judaism, and Islam. In the Middle East, the stranger is considered "a messenger from God." I repeated these mandates a few times, and one Sunday after the service, the congregation voted to open the doors of Luther Place to all creatures great and small in whatever condition. On Monday night, we welcomed the strangers, opening God's doors and extending the biblical invitation "come unto me …" In twenty-four hours, we were wall to wall with the holy family of homeless thawing out in stairwells, in the social hall, even classrooms and the chapel. There is an efficient communications network on the streets. In came the poorest of the poor, the sickest of the sick, people infested with lice and scabies, paranoid schizophrenics, tubercular, and the unbathed crowded our floors, carrying the few things they owned in bags or carts. The church literally reeked of homelessness. Metropolitan Washington was stunned by this congregational action. But it was done! The faithful people of Luther Place opened the doors. We as a church had to make the biblical choice. The Bible says "Choose life, not death. Be a blessing, not a curse." Hallways, stairwells, the chapel, the social hall, and classrooms became "the Church as refuge!" After 1976, there was no turning back. The homeless issue was squarely in our face … The mission of Luther Place was hospitality, welcoming the stranger. It was a gradual enlightenment that came along the road.

Martin Marty, in his book *Collision of Faiths*, says that fundamentalism in America came with fear of the "threat of the stranger"—that is, the influx of immigrants from different cultures and religions. Rather than welcoming strangers, which is biblical tradition, fundamentalists try to wall themselves off from strangers and often try to push restrictive policies on them.

The Christian message, centered on the gospel of Jesus, is much more about seeking justice than about the narrow cultural agenda of the religious-right (largely white evangelical) leaders in America. It never made sense to many followers of Jesus that evangelicals would put homosexuality and abortion at the forefront of their religious crusade. Jesus never even talked about these issues in the gospels, whereas he did talk overwhelmingly about serving the vulnerable in society, *the least of these*. Issues such as homosexuality have been widely debated and taken to the highest levels of our nation's legal system and are now settled law. So where does that leave the Christian evangelical movement in America? Some key voices among evangelicals have warned that if white Christianity continues to stand with the forces of exclusion and hate in America it is doomed for oblivion. This would apply to political parties and their leaders as well.

What I see today is a need for rejuvenation of a more progressive and inclusive spirit in America to counter the more fundamentalist trends that, if followed, would take us back to a period before the 1960s civil rights movement, when the white majority was dominant, women were expected to be homemakers, and minorities were openly oppressed. Many young people have turned away from organized religion, but there is a large spirituality movement that has much in common with more traditional progressive church values. Many are turned off by members of the religious right, who have captured too much of the current religious media's attention with such negative rhetoric. Those in the progressive religious community need to find ways to connect with today's spiritual movement, social justice–oriented evangelicals, and secular progressives. We have the great examples of the Social Gospel movement and Catholic social teaching, which played influential roles in the progressive search for economic fairness and justice in the early part of the twentieth century. Both traditions promoted the belief that any true commitment to scripture demanded that followers take concrete steps to address oppression and hardship in this world. Where and when will the prophetic voices and leaders arise in our nation, the present-day equivalents of Frederick Douglass, Dorothy Day, Dr. Martin Luther King, Jr.?

There is increasing recognition of a transformation going on in religion, says Harvey Cox in his book *The Future of Faith.* He says that religious people are increasingly more interested in spiritual disciplines than in doctrines. The result is a universal trend away from hierarchical, patriarchal, and institutional religion. As these changes gain momentum, they evoke an almost point-for-point fundamentalist reaction. Fundamentalism, Cox argues, is on graphic display around the globe because it is dying. Cox says this recent move away from dogmatic religion is best explained against the backdrop of three distinct periods of church history:

1. **The Age of Faith.** For the first three centuries of Christianity, the early church was more concerned with following Jesus's teachings than with enforcing what to believe.
2. **The Age of Belief.** From the fourth to the twentieth century, the church focused on orthodoxy and doctrine.

3. **The Age of the Spirit.** A trend that began in the last half century or so and that is increasingly moving the church away from dogma and toward breaking down barriers between different religions and spirituality is increasingly replacing formal religion.

In one of his examples about the Age of Belief, Cox cites the "The Great Schism"—the great divide between Western and Eastern Christianity that split the church in 1054. One of the key issues that led to this split was a theological question concerning internal relationships within what is referred to as the "godhead" (God, the Son, and the Holy Spirit or the Trinity). More specifically, the question revolved around whether the Holy Spirit proceeds from the Father and the Son, which was the position of the Western church, or from the Father only, which was the position of the Eastern church. This disagreement leads one to ask, how on earth could we possibly know about the internal relations of the godhead? Isn't it finally time to put this silly schism and other such religious divides behind us and focus on what is important, putting faith into action?

Dietrich Bonhoeffer, like Cox, made the distinction between faith and institutional religion. In his prison letters, Bonhoeffer mused about the emergence of a "religionless Christianity." Having witnessed the complete failure of the German Protestant church as an institution in the face of Nazism, he saw this challenge as an opportunity of renewal for Christianity.[8] Further, Bonhoeffer said with regard to justice, "We are not to simply bandage the wounds of victims beneath

> **Bonhoeffer says about justice,** "We are not to simply bandage the wounds of victims beneath the wheels of injustice, we are to drive a spoke into the wheel itself."

the wheels of injustice, we are to drive a spoke into the wheel itself."[9]

As mentioned at the beginning of this chapter, there are many important social and political issues at both the local and national levels that desperately need a progressive, social justice–oriented action agenda that brings together the faithful, spiritual, and secular justice-oriented communities. We like to think of our country as particularly blessed by God and exceptional among nations. Yet a recent report evaluating social justice among developed countries shows the United States to be in the lower tier of countries on justice indicators, particularly due to our country's high poverty levels.[10] Economic justice is an increasingly important issue, as the growing gap in income between the wealthy and the average worker threatens the American dream. Further, the tendency for federal and state budget cuts to be targeted at programs helping society's most vulnerable needs to be much more aggressively challenged by both secular and religious progressives.

Pope Francis's new 300-page encyclical in October 2020, *Fratelli Tutti*, outlines his recommendations for rebuilding a post-pandemic world, beginning with a complete restructuring of politics and civil discourse in order to create systems prioritizing the community and the poor, rather than individual or market interests. He says that "we believers need to find occasions to speak with one another and to act together for the common good and the promotion of the poor." The Pope calls for care of the marginalized, support for migrants, resistance of nationalism and populism, and the abolition of the death penalty. Pope Francis said that leaders should focus on the long-term common good, instilling their work with what he called "political love." He repeats his frequent criticisms of populism and free-market capitalism, voicing support for multilateral efforts and policies that prioritize the most vulnerable, including migrants and refugees. He also appeals for women's rights and equality, urges a widespread defense of the elderly, and an urgent end to racism.

To further advance social justice and the common good in Washington, DC, Luther Place founded N Street Village (NSV) in 1972, aimed at nourishing the impoverished and homeless in the city. As I will discuss in later chapters, NSV is now the largest provider of services and housing to homeless and formerly homeless adult women in DC. Luther Place then founded the Lutheran Volunteer Corps (LVC) some forty years ago, in 1979.[11] It is modeled after the Jesuit Volunteer Corp and the Mennonite Volunteer Corp, which place yearlong volunteers (normally recent college graduates) in social justice ministries dealing with poverty, housing, homelessness, environmental concerns, immigration and refugees, and a variety of other challenging justice issues. This experience exposes young people to life-giving programs for vulnerable people and is often formative in their vocation decisions. The LVC still has its headquarters at Luther Place, and it now places volunteers in up to ten US cities each year. Over three thousand young people have graduated from the LVC, and many have gone on to become pastors or doctors or to work in nonprofit social justice programs around the country. Others may go into business or public service, and the experience instills a culture of justice and the common good in their career and volunteer pursuits.

Yet another program of Luther Place that exposes young people to issues such as poverty and homelessness is the Steinbruck Center.[12] The Steinbruck Center provides transformative, urban immersion experiences for groups of young people through a combination of education, direct service, experiential learning, critical analysis, and reflection. It takes them on a social justice journey by providing opportunities and spaces for meaningful service and mutual transformation. The program, which serves over a thousand young people each year, inspires participants to engage in self-reflection and become agents of change to address root causes of poverty in their home communities.

Other recent community programs initiated by Luther Place include:

- The **Beloved Community Incubator,** a nonprofit that supports worker-owned cooperatives and social enterprises with a vision for racial and economic equity. Worker co-ops create quality jobs and real change for often marginalized workers in their communities. In 2018, the incubator launched its first cooperative, Dulce Hogar Cleaning Cooperative, in which Latina immigrant women in the increasingly upscale Fourteenth Street corridor of DC are empowered to operate their own business rather than work at low wages for other corporate entities.

- **ArtSmart Summer Camp** was established in 2012 in response to the need for affordable summer camps in the Logan Circle neighborhood. ArtSmart Summer Camp is a community arts-based summer program run for a period of four weeks for approximately 40 young people (1st through 6th grade). In 2016, the Middle School Leadership Program was established for 7th and 8th graders. Campers experience a weekly theme through music, drama, art, and games, as well as spending afternoons engaging physical activity. In 2020 the program was challenged by the pandemic but was able to do class offerings online and provided weekly deliveries of needed food and other supplies to families through Ward 2 DC COVID-19 Mutual Aid.

Hospitality Center for Protestors was established in 2020 in support of BLM and associated protestors in DC much of which occurred only blocks from the church. The hospitality center at Luther Place offered water, refreshments, masks, basic first aid, bathrooms, and such during active protest periods. While others boarded up their windows, locked their doors and turned off the lights in the midst of the protests, a large group of Luther Place leaders and volunteers opened doors to those who needed it. It was mostly a peaceful environment over those months, but several racist incidents occurred leading up to the January 6 assault on the Capitol. Our BLM banner was torn down multiple times by a white supremacist contingent and they burned BLM banners at two neighboring churches in December. On Wednesday morning, January 6, an interfaith group of religious leaders gathered outside Luther Place, standing for an end to violence, for an eradication of white nationalism, and for a groundswell of racial justice. During their prayer service, men adorned in patriotic clothing and "Make America Great Again" hats approached. One walked into the middle of the circle, pretended to fall, and laid on the ground while another man knelt on his neck mocking the 2020 killing of George Floyd at the hands of police. These were truly despicable acts on sacred ground and were a sad precursor to the armed invasion of the Capitol later in the day. It is a day that will go down in infamy as home grown terrorists encouraged by then President Trump attacked our precious seat of power resulting in mass destruction, injuries, and deaths.

3

Economic Opportunity

In many comparisons of developed countries, the US ranks near the top, most notably in its economic power. It also is remarkable in its historic ability to absorb so many cultures, making it the great "melting pot"; we are the most diverse and inclusive nation on earth. The US historically has been widely perceived as the great land of opportunity. An astounding statistic showing how our country benefits from immigrants is that one-quarter of the members of our National Academy of Sciences were born abroad. We have the top universities in the world, which attract these best minds. But several studies of what makes a country great have shown that the US, despite having a robust economy, also has higher economic inequality than most competitors, and this has increased in recent decades. According to the Congressional Research Service (using cross-sectional data collected from the Current Population Survey), overall wages rose significantly in real terms over the 1979 to 2018 period at the top of the wage distribution (37.6 percent for the 90th percentile, or top 10 percent), increased more modestly at the middle of the wage distribution (6.1 percent at the 50th percentile), and rose to an even lesser degree at the bottom of the distribution (1.6 percent for the 10th percentile).[13] Women experienced significant wage growth while men actually lost ground in the middle and lower groups (i.e., a 25.7 percent gain for women and a 5.1 percent loss for men at the 50th percentile). Wage rates also have been significantly affected by education level and race, as will be discussed further in this chapter. A recent study by Oren Cass at the Manhattan Institute shows that in our current economy, a middle-class adult can no longer provide middle-class security to a family, as might have been the case in the 1980s.[14] Wages have increased modestly since then, but costs for housing, education, health, and other family expenses have risen faster. And the racial economic disparities are dramatic. For example, Federal Reserve data showed that African American families' median net worth was $17,600 in 2016, versus $171,000 for white households, a tenfold difference. Nearly one-fifth of Black families have zero or negative net worth — twice the rate of white families.[15] And according to the Census Bureau, in the fourth quarter of 2019, 44 percent of African Americans owned homes, down four percentage points from 2007, just before the last recession. The white homeownership rate was 74 percent in 2019, virtually the same as in 2007.

As I write, the world and our nation are experiencing a pandemic that is having serious economic impacts, particularly on the most vulnerable. Global GDP for 2020 is expected by leading economists to drop at least 4 percent which would be the worst since World War II. In a bit over a decade under the Obama and Trump administrations, the US economy had added over 20 million jobs since the Great Recession. In a matter of weeks, all those gains vanished as more than that number of workers were pushed into unemployment. This only compounded existing economic vulnerabilities and inequalities among so many families and individuals. For example, only 47 percent of private-sector workers in the bottom quarter for wages have paid sick leave, compared with 90 percent in the top quarter, according to the Economic Policy Institute. Faced suddenly with the pandemic, Congress was able to provide much-needed short term relief with a large economic stimulus and benefit package, but more is still needed and what will happen when the crisis passes? Do we want to go back to our broken political system? Are we willing to have governments and corporations return to business as usual, where the money seems to flow upward? Do we want to go back to the economic situation where sick employees are forced to take unpaid leave or work while sick if they want to keep their jobs? Do we want to continue to have 30 million people without health care coverage? Do we want to accept cities cutting off services or evicting their poorest residents or throwing someone in jail because the person cannot afford to pay a fine? Do we go back to denigrating people if they need public assistance? I believe we should follow the call that President Franklin D. Roosevelt issued to the country during the Great Depression: "We now realize as we have never realized before our interdependence on each other; that we cannot merely take but we must give as well; that if we are to go forward, we must move as a trained and loyal army willing to sacrifice for the good of a common discipline."

US Economy at a Glance

Overall, there are many positives about the US economy. It is the world's largest in nominal GDP and the second largest in purchasing power parity. The US has a highly diversified, world-leading industrial sector. It is also a high-technology innovator. The US dollar is the currency most used in international transactions and is the world's foremost reserve currency. The nation's economy is fueled by abundant natural resources, a well-developed infrastructure, and relatively high productivity, although its rate of growth has declined in recent decades. Of the world's 500 largest companies, 134 are headquartered in the United States. The US also has one of the world's largest and most influential financial markets, including the New York Stock Exchange, which is by far the world's largest stock exchange by market capitalization.

The Federal Reserve's Annual Survey of Household Economics and Decision-Making, conducted in 2019 prior to the pandemic, presented a picture of improving financial well-being among Americans since 2013, the first year of the survey.[16] When asked about their finances, 75 percent of adults said they were either doing okay or living comfortably. The result in 2018 was similar to 2017, standing at twelve percentage points higher than 2013. Although their finances had improved substantially, a sizable share of adults still said that they would struggle with a modest unexpected expense. If faced with an unexpected expense of $400, 61 percent of adults said they would cover it with cash, savings, or a credit card paid off at the next statement. Similar to the prior year, 27 percent would borrow or sell something to pay for the expense, and 12 percent would not be able to cover the expense at all. Overall, the survey showed that three in ten adults either were unable to pay all their bills or were one modest financial setback away from hardship. Further, the survey reported that one-fourth of adults had skipped necessary medical care in 2018 because they were unable to afford the cost. So, although the economy had improved considerably since the Great Recession, there was still considerable financial vulnerability among US households. And then in 2020, the country suddenly entered into a new recession triggered by the coronavirus pandemic. This caused major disruptions for employees and businesses across much of the economy. Without doubt, the pandemic has exacerbated the financial uncertainty in already vulnerable households and put many more at risk. The Congressional Research Service's November 2020 household economic update says based on an experimental U.S. Census Bureau household survey fielded to track the implications of the pandemic, "The Census survey found that close to half of all households in the United States experienced at least some loss of employment income since March 2020, when the economic effects of the pandemic first became apparent…While employment income loss was widespread, it was disproportionately in households that were in lower income categories in 2019 and households with children under age 18." [17] There was a higher concentration of losses among minorities and women were more impacted than men. For example, the US Bureau of Labor Statistics reported that of the nearly 1.1 million people who stopped working or were looking for work in September 2020, 80 percent were women; an illustration of the childcare burden for working mothers as remote schooling began. Analysts suggest this has been a most unequal recession as the sectors most deeply affected by COVID disproportionately employ women, minorities, and lower-income workers. Compounding the economic impact, the coronavirus pandemic is having profound psychological effects as well.

Global Comparisons

U.S. News & World Report, with the BAV Group and Wharton School, has conducted a "Best Countries" survey since 2016.[18] The United States ranked number eight overall in the 2019 survey. Though the US is seen as the most powerful country in the world and scored highly for its entrepreneurship and cultural influence, its ranking was affected by the sharpest drop in global trust among all countries assessed since 2016. The dimensions considered were sixty-five wide-ranging attributes covering economic, social, environmental, and institutional factors. The US, the world's greatest military power and largest economy, ranked high in many factors, including its openness and diversity. The factors pulling the US down compared to competitors included education and job readiness, economic and social inequality, environmental concerns, and health and public safety.

According to an international index, the OECD Better Life Index (note: The Organization for Economic Cooperation and Development, OECD, has not assigned an overall ranking to countries), the United States performs very well in many measures of well-being relative to most other developed countries. The US ranks at the top in housing, income, and wealth but has a considerable economic gap between the richest and poorest citizens in comparison with competitors. It ranks above average but not among the very highest in health status, job security, education and job skills, social connections, personal security, subjective well-being, environmental quality, and civic engagement.

So, despite being a country of great opportunity, the United States clearly has ways in which it can improve. Entrepreneurship in the US is judged to be excellent by the OECD Index, but economic inequality is high, and many low- to middle-income workers are feeling left behind. A major competitor, Germany, provides some positive examples to look at with its small- and medium-business development and job-readiness efforts through apprenticeships. Germany also provides better childcare and other family- and gender-friendly work policies. Regarding health, education, and social well-being, the high US spending on health care compared to outcomes is an area identified for improvement in the US compared to key OECD competitors. Higher-education affordability is increasingly an issue for many in our country. On questions about life satisfaction and happiness, the Scandinavian countries excelled in these surveys; we could learn a bit from them on such issues. Work–family balance is one such area. Americans work longer hours than workers in most other developed countries, yet they do so with fewer benefits (like sick/family leave and childcare) to support working families and this became even more painfully obvious during the pandemic.

Effects of Economic Globalization

Each year in Davos, Switzerland, around three thousand of the world's elites from the arenas of business, finance, politics, and public affairs gather for the World Economic Forum, with the goal of addressing global challenges. The theme of the 2019 gathering was "Responsive and Responsible Leadership," and its objectives emphasized that growth must be inclusive and sustainable, likely responding to the populist shake-up happening in many advanced countries. In a book about global economic disparities, *Winners Take All: The Elite Charade of Changing the World*, journalist Anand Giridharadas takes on the global elite class who gather at Davos and such global venues. He says that America and other parts of the world have seen tremendous technological innovation spurred by global companies, but the benefits seem to accrue mostly upward, as the top 10 percent hold about 90 percent of the world's wealth. He suggests that it is now clear that globalization, technology, and market liberalization did not bring their promised benefits for the majority of working Americans or for the working class in other advanced countries. He further questions the system that allows elite business leaders to make their money, often in predatory ways, and then try to compensate for that through philanthropy. Giridharadas mentions the Sackler family and their pharmaceutical empire that helped make them one of America's wealthiest and most philanthropic families; as we now know, they also spurred and profited off America's opioid crisis, prompting investigations by the US Department of Justice.

Giridharadas and others suggest that the world's billionaire charitable donors committing to giving away a portion of their wealth is not going to save the world; it may ease their conscience, but it does little overall to help the vast problem of economic inequality. Giridharadas says his is not an anti-globalist view, but one that recognizes the key role of national governments and their basic responsibility for the social and economic well-being of their citizens. This responsibility, he says, cannot be supplanted by multinational economic entities such as the World Trade Organization (WTO), the International Monetary Fund (IMF), the World Economic Forum, the European Union (EU), and others. In the case of the UK and its Brexit challenge, the EU elites bear some responsibility for the national populist backlash in the UK and in multiple European countries. Citizens often feel they have no voice in these multinational institutions that are making the economic rules that affect their lives. And since the US Supreme Court's *Citizens United* decision opened the doors to wealthy individual and corporate campaign donors, the economic elite's influence has further increased at the expense of the average US voter.

Dani Rodrik, an economist at Harvard who writes about globalization, says that global elites speak grandly of improving the world but largely insulate themselves from the rest of society, unlike many US companies that once felt themselves part of local communities where they were then headquartered. Rodrik says that global elites dislike nationalism and promote globalization, and he further suggests that they are more inclined to focus their attention on developing-world issues than to tackle the problems of declining industries in the Rust Belt of the United States. He believes that 2016 presidential candidate Clinton's association with the global elites was a contributor to her detachment from the working-class electorate, although her policies might well have been better for them. In the end, critics suggest that rather than relying on 'scraps' from the global winners we must take on the democratic work of building more robust governmental institutions and economies in each nation.

In the spring of 2020, the COVID-19 outbreak generated both demand and supply shocks that reverberated across the global economy and the markets. We experienced a sudden recession that further contributed to economic and social disruption. COVID-19 is dramatically affecting industries across much of the globe, and the outbreak is likely to result in longer-lasting reconfigurations of supply chains to build resilience. This is already under way as some US companies diversify away from heavy reliance on goods from Asia. And maybe consumers will become a bit less materialistic; our hyperactive consumer society has provided more material goods than many need to lead a sustainable life.

The following sections look at recent economic trends in the United States and some of the demographic and geographic factors underlying those trends.

Demographic and Geographic Economic Challenges

Nearly 35 percent of rural counties in the United States are experiencing significant population loss, according to 2019 research released by the Carsey School of Public Policy at the University of New Hampshire.[19] The researchers found that 746 counties representing 24 percent of all US counties are depopulating, and 91 percent of them are rural. This population loss is disproportionately among younger adults. As youth have continued to migrate from rural areas to cities, their movement has widened the gap in median age and birth rate between rural places and cities and has affected community dynamism provided by younger age groups, whose outlook tends to be more worldly and embracing of diversity. In the last decade or so of economic recovery, more than 95 percent of all job and population growth went to metropolitan areas. There are places in the country where the recession of more than a decade ago never ended. Rural, remote places have been disproportionately losing not just jobs and opportunities, but people, elementary schools, and confidence in the future. Small farms are also disappearing further decimating rural counties. For example, the Agriculture Department reports that the overall number of licensed dairy farms in the US declined by more than 50 percent from 2003 to 2019. And many amenities taken for granted in big cities are all but absent in many rural communities. Rural counties near metropolitan areas tend to be the exception to the widespread rural population loss, given the economic advantages of metropolitan proximity. Rural counties with major recreation attractions also tend to buck the trend.

Factory jobs that were often the mainstay of small-town America are no longer that. Even after a robust growth in manufacturing output in the last decade, there are fewer than 13 million workers in manufacturing across the entire economy. Both technology and globalization have reduced domestic manufacturing jobs, and those manufacturing jobs that remain often demand higher skills. The emerging high-tech industries today do not have much need for the relatively unskilled cheap labor that rural communities provided during America's industrial past. In their new book, *Deaths of Despair and the Future of Capitalism*, Anne Case and Angus Deaton paint a troubling portrait of the American dream in decline for America's working class. They say, "For the white working class, today's America has become a land of broken families and few prospects. As the college educated become healthier and wealthier, adults without a degree are literally dying from pain and despair." Capitalism, which lifted so many people out of poverty in the last century, is now leaving blue-collar America behind.

The US economic base has shifted in ways that benefit major metropolitan areas at the expense of smaller cities and rural communities. Our technology-driven economy is now based much more on knowledge and idea exchange than on the material product connections of the twentieth-century manufacturing economy. Globalization and rapid spread of technology such as the internet and mass media have facilitated this shift. The previous century's industrial economy was more locally interconnected, with factories employing local workers, making goods from local raw materials to be sold locally, and being financed and managed locally. The industrial economy spread its benefits across a wide region. For example, Chicago served as a regional hub, interconnecting many smaller cities in a multistate Midwest manufacturing region, but that regional economic interconnection seems to be fracturing with the evolution of the global technological economy.

By contrast, the global technology-driven economy benefits key US megacity regions (upward of twenty-five) that might be called the globally connected cities, which account for 40 to 50 percent of the US population but a significantly higher percentage of the nation's economic growth. The global economy is based on flow of information, goods, money, jobs, and people, around the world. A city thrives today less because of what it makes locally than because of where it stands in the global supply chain. The emerging economy values college degrees, technical specialties, and entrepreneurialism, which attracts young, educated workers. This has enabled several "elite" cities to surge ahead of the rest of the country in their wealth and income.

It seems that once a metropolitan area attracts key innovative workers and companies, its economy changes in ways that make it even more attractive to other innovators. But the increasingly high housing prices in these areas are leading to growth in a host of second-tier cities. Seattle has benefited from this trend, and the Denver/Boulder region is an emerging metro area where tech workers can enjoy a combination of lower home costs and good urban and outdoor amenities. A few old industrial cities such as Pittsburgh have made the transition to the new economy with the support of leading-edge research universities, such as Carnegie Mellon and its artificial intelligence program. The San Francisco Bay area deserves special mention among these technology-leading regions. The world's most valuable tech company, Apple, is anchored in Silicon Valley along with other tech leaders such as Google, Facebook, and Uber. The Apple economic model is similar to that of other tech companies. Their knowledge base and idea generation are in California while their tech products are mostly made in China. So, Silicon Valley's technology–industry link is more to China than to other smaller cities in the US, as might have been the case in the old manufacturing model. A parallel trend since the 1980s has been corporate mergers and creation of giant companies, many of them global. Meanwhile, many small businesses have struggled to keep up with the new corporate giants and with foreign competition; local family-owned stores and small manufacturing establishments are largely disappearing.

Although technology innovation tends to cluster in major cities with the needed skilled labor force (illustrated by Amazon in its decision to locate a major new office in the Washington, DC, area), we also need to stimulate economic development in medium-sized communities. Targeted economic incentives focused on promising middle-sized communities that have resources like a community college, other critical infrastructure, and reasonable access to a larger regional technology hub may offer promise. Also, recent agricultural research finds that although small farms are disappearing, there is potential in midsize farm operations that may be pivotal to helping regional agriculture reach a meaningful scale. The "Ag of the Middle" program funded by the Department of Agriculture focuses investment incentives on value-added farm operations that have the greatest likelihood of being sustainable. It is clear that not every small town or city can be revived, but strategically creating key hubs of economic promise can improve the outlook for rural America. And possibly in the aftermath of the pandemic, remote work may free up more workers to live where they want. We could see some workers leaving the New York's and San Francisco's of the country and moving to smaller and cheaper cities like Austin, Salt Lake, or Raleigh-Durham or to resort areas. There is much speculation and some anecdotal evidence since COVID-19, but it is too early to see how large this trend will be.

There are also some gender-related social and economic trends that are hindering economic progress. Girls in recent years have overtaken boys at virtually every stage of education, with higher grades from the early years through high school and college. Men are now a minority on college campuses, accounting for just over 40 percent of graduates. The greater success among girls and young women seems to relate to more self-discipline and focused study habits. Boys and young men seem more likely to be distracted by the likes of video games and by heavier drinking and drug use. With a better education and more skills, women have advanced steadily in the workplace; women have moved into formerly all-male jobs in fields such as law, business, and medicine. American women are now almost as likely to work outside the home as men, but the glass ceiling is far from being shattered. Women still make up only 27 percent of the top 10 percent of labor income earners, and their share in higher-income groups is even smaller. Among the top 1 percent, women make up slightly less than 17 percent of workers, while at the top 0.1 percent level, they make up only 11 percent according to the Economic Policy Institute.[20] The COVID-19 pandemic and its economic fallout has unfortunately impacted women more than men given their predominant role with childcare responsibilities and the recovery implications are still uncertain.

The world in which high-paid manufacturing jobs for men could support a family and where women were expected to focus only on being wives and mothers is largely gone. Women have made the transition to a changing economy in recent decades better than men. The share of prime-age men—those twenty-five to fifty-four years old—who are not working has more than tripled since the late 1960s, and it has become harder for men to find higher-paying jobs. Foreign competition and technological advances have eliminated many of the blue-collar manufacturing jobs in which high school graduates once could earn upward of $40 an hour. A high proportion of these prime-age men without jobs do not have bachelor's degrees.

According to a report released by the Council of Economic Advisers (CEA) in June 2016, in the half century between 1965 and 2015, employment rates for prime working-age American males spiraled downward, with an ever-growing number of working-age men not present in the labor force based on Bureau of Labor Statistics data.[21] At that time, a bit over 15 percent of working-age men in America were either unemployed or out of the workforce altogether, and the most recent data show that number is still in that range. A perplexing fact is that this phenomenon seems to be much more prevalent in America than in other developed economies. Data show that these non-working prime-age men skew toward younger ages, are largely unmarried, are disproportionately less educated, and tend to be concentrated in Appalachia, the Rust Belt, and the Deep South. A disproportionate number are African American, likely related to the effects of mass incarceration in recent decades. It should be noted that in this same time period, women have greatly increased in the workforce, so our total workforce overall has grown dramatically. This growth of women in the workforce in recent decades tended to mask the disappearance of so many men from active work.

Using mortality data from the Centers for Disease Control and Prevention (CDC) and from other sources, Princeton economists, Angus Deaton and Anne Case, discovered rising annual death rates among this economically disadvantaged middle-age group of white men with a high school education or less.[22] The higher death rates are being driven not so much by traditional killers such as heart disease, stroke, and diabetes but by significantly higher rates of suicide and afflictions stemming from substance and alcohol abuse and overdoses of heroin and prescription drugs. Since 1999, in this lower-educated group of white males, death rates rose by over 20 percent, while death rates actually fell for those with a college education. Economic stress for the traditional blue-collar working class almost certainly is playing a role. Many are falling short of the American dream as they reach midlife. Median real household incomes for whites with a high school education have fallen since the late 1990s. Their study update, released in 2017, extends the data by two years and shows that the trend is continuing. Deaton and Case concluded that,

> less-educated white Americans who struggle in the job market in early adulthood are likely to experience a 'cumulative disadvantage' over time, with health and personal problems that often lead to drug overdoses, alcohol-related liver disease and suicide … ultimately, we see our story as about the collapse of the white, high-school-educated working class after its heyday in the early 1970s, and the pathologies that accompany that decline.

The CDC shows a drop in US life expectancy in recent years, primarily attributed to drug addiction and suicide rising fast among younger adults, particularly men. The average life span of an American had risen for decades, reaching 78.9 years in 2014. But it took a dip in 2015, held steady in 2016, dipped again in 2017, and slightly improved to 78.7 years in 2018 and 78.8 years in 2019 still below the 2014 level. This pullback in life expectancy improvement is largely driven by the steep growth in drug overdose and suicide deaths. According to the CDC, over 47,000 Americans died from suicide during 2017, which is higher in both number and percentage of the population than at any time since the CDC's earliest published statistics in 1950. Today, there are two suicides for every homicide death and 17 percent more suicide deaths per year than deaths from motor vehicle incidents. Suicide affects all ages and demographic groups, but men between the ages of forty-five and sixty-four make up the biggest number of suicides, with some 12,000 suicide deaths in 2017. The group represents about 6 percent of the population but accounts for more than a quarter of the suicides; the rate is up 45 percent since 1999. Most of the suicides in this middle-aged group have involved guns, a method that is almost always lethal.

As mentioned previously regarding urban versus rural economic opportunities, the Princeton authors showed that mortality rates declined in major cities and were constant in the suburbs but rose in rural areas. The CDC published a report on US suicides by level of urbanization between 1999 and 2015.[23] The report shows rising suicide rates as urbanization decreased and indicates that this urban–rural divide appears to have widened in recent years.

In a 2016 National Institutes of Health paper titled *Family Inequality: Diverging Patterns in Marriage, Cohabitation, and Childbearing*, the authors explain a cycle that is increasingly separating lower-educated Americans from upwardly mobile college-educated individuals and families.[24] The declining employment and salaries of men without college degrees make them less attractive as marriage partners. The result, according to the authors, is "a decoupling of marriage and childbearing," with larger percentages of children brought up in single-mother households. Children in single-parent households typically inherit multiple disadvantages that schools in many cases cannot overcome.

In contrast, for those with at least a bachelor's degree, the authors suggest, "marriage has become the commitment device that supports intensive joint investments in children," a project for "raising economically-successful children." These parents provide intensive investments in children such as increased childcare time, early reading support, early preschool enrollment, enrollment in many extracurricular activities, and the like. The children therefore come into a school environment with many more advantages over lower-income students, and this continues throughout their developmental period. Thus, children from poor and working-class homes are often doubly disadvantaged, first by meager economic resources and second by the fact that they are in single-parent families, which often means fewer support systems. By contrast, children from more educated and affluent homes are doubly advantaged by their parents' substantial economic resources and by the fact that their parents usually get and stay married.

Political promises to bring back old manufacturing industries to boost employment for working-class men ring hollow in the face of a global economy and technological change. A much more robust discussion across the political divide is needed to understand the forces at work and to help formulate policies that could actually work for many of these families. The decline of labor unions has also reduced workers' control of their economic situations, as has the increased prevalence of so-called right-to-work laws—which allow employees covered by union contracts to avoid paying dues while still requiring unions to absorb the costs of representing them. Unions now represent less than 7 percent of the workforce. The COVID-19 pandemic in 2020, highlighted an additional lack of benefit for US workers—paid sick leave—and this exacerbated the economic impacts of the pandemic.

There is no easy solution to these trends. Many economic analysts converge around a core set of policies, including short-term job retraining to help displaced manufacturing workers enter the emerging economy and family economic benefits such as childcare and family leave, which are considered basic benefits that any advanced society should have. Advocates also push for improved education of our students, with more emphasis on science and math preparation (STEM). After all, this is the future workforce for the emerging twenty-first-century technological and service economy. And we can help ensure a better future by investing today in important economic stimulus areas such as advanced educational opportunities, renewed infrastructure, and scientific research and development.

Economic Inequality

Many worry that we have entered another Gilded Age like that of the early twenty-first century as we see growing extremes in economic inequality. There are two key aspects of economic inequality: wealth inequality and income inequality. Regarding wealth inequality, economist Edward Wolff's 2017 analysis shows that wealth inequality is higher than it has been in more than fifty years.[25] Analyses by the Federal Reserve[26] and the Pew Research Center reach similar conclusions. Their research finds that the wealthiest 1 percent of American households own nearly 40 percent of the country's wealth, and they own more wealth than the bottom 90 percent combined! A similar analysis done by Inequality.org using National Bureau of Economic Research data shows that the richest 5 percent of Americans own two-thirds of all wealth, the top 1 percent own nearly

40 percent (consistent with aforementioned Federal Reserve and Pew Research findings), and the bottom 90 percent of Americans own only about 20 percent of all wealth, as shown in the figure here[27].

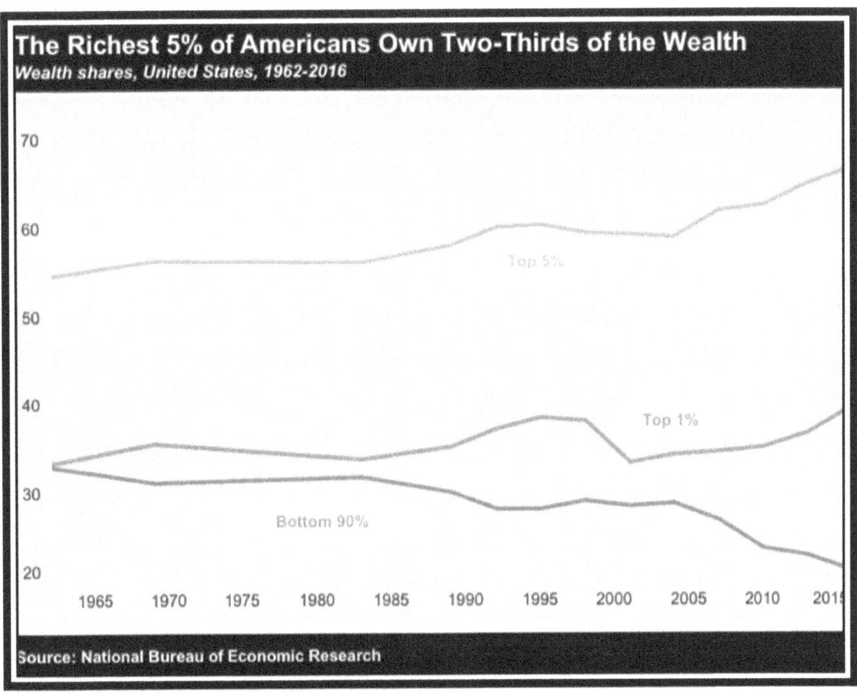

Wealth shares in America (by Inequality.org using National Bureau of Economic Research data)

No wonder there is economic discord in our country. Since the great recession in 2007, high-income households have gained wealth, while middle- and lower-income households have lost it. Pew Research Center reported that in 2016, the median wealth of lower-income families was 42 percent less than in 2007, and the median wealth of middle-income families was 33 percent lower. This put middle- and lower-income families back to levels equivalent to those in 1989.[28] Distressingly, the share of the nation's households with no or negative net worth has risen to over 20 percent. And the wealth disparity by race is significant; according to Pew Research, lower-income white households had a net worth of $22,900 in 2016, compared with only $5,000 for Black households and $7,900 for Hispanic households in this income tier. A significant factor of wealth loss for middle- and lower-income families was the housing bust in the 2007–2009 period and its slow recovery since. Nearly 10 million homeowners lost their homes to foreclosure sales in the US between 2006 and 2014, caused by subprime mortgages and the like promulgated by lenders. Meanwhile, high-income households have seen record stock prices increase their wealth dramatically in the last decade. The Federal Reserve confirmed these trends in a recent report, saying that at the end of 2018, the average middle-income household had wealth of about $340,000, while the average household in the top 10 percent of the income distribution had wealth of about $4.5 million.[29] The average wealth of the top-income decile is now thirteen times higher than that of the middle-income group, whereas it was seven times higher in 1989. Newly released Federal Reserve data show sadly that the net worth of White Americans hit a record high in 2020, driven by a stock-market rebound that defied the pandemic, while Blacks and other minorities saw their share of the nation's wealth decline. The United States seems to be an outlier in this extreme wealth inequality among the world's advanced economies. The top 1 percent in the US own twice as much as in countries like France, Britain, and Canada. There is concern that we are moving toward another Gilded Age similar to what the country experienced in the late nineteenth century.

Regarding income inequality, in the mid-1970s the top 1 percent earned 10.5 percent of the total national income, and the bottom half earned 20 percent. By 2015, those percentages had effectively flipped, with most estimates showing the top

1 percent earning just over a 20 percent share and the bottom half dropping to 12.5 percent of national income. In September 2019, the Census Bureau reported that income inequality in the United States had hit its highest level in 2018 since the Census Bureau started tracking it more than five decades ago.[30] The federal minimum wage has stood at $7.25 for well over a decade, and this is one of the reasons the gap between the rich and poor is widening. Census data showed that in 2018, over half (52 percent) of all money income went to the wealthiest fifth of the population, as shown in the following breakdown by quintile group. Yet the Trump administration's last budget submission included about $2 trillion in cuts to safety-net programs, including reductions affecting Medicaid, federal housing assistance, and food stamps. Unfortunately, the COVID-19 economic recession again disproportionately impacted lower income households while the economically advantaged comfortably worked from their homes via technology.

US Money Income Share by Income Quintile
(2018 Bureau of Census)

- Lowest quintile: 3.1 percent
- Second quintile: 8.3 percent
- Third quintile: 14.1 percent
- Fourth quintile: 22.6 percent
- Highest quintile: 52.0 percent (note: top 5 percent share is 23.1 percent)

Thomas Piketty, in his 2014 book *Capital in the Twenty-First Century*, highlights the dramatic rise of the income shares of the top 10 percent and the top 1 percent (with special emphasis on the top 0.1 percent). Piketty's colleague Emmanuel Saez, an economics professor at UC-Berkeley, confirms these results. According to Saez's research, US income inequality has been increasing steadily since the 1970s and now has reached levels not seen since 1928. Using tax return data from the IRS, Saez has built extensive income-distribution data sets going back one hundred years. His analysis shows that in 1928, the top 1 percent of families received about 24 percent of all pretax income, while the bottom 90 percent received just over 50 percent. But the Depression and World War II dramatically reshaped the nation's income distribution, and by 1944 the top 1 percent's share was down to just over 11 percent, while the bottom 90 percent were receiving about two-thirds, and that stayed relatively constant for the next three decades. But starting in the mid- to late 1970s, the uppermost tier's income share began rising dramatically, while that of the bottom 90 percent started to fall, so that now we are almost back to the 1928 levels of income inequality.[31] Saez's research further showed that the top 1 percent of families captured half of all real income growth in the economic recovery between 2009 and 2017, with the top 1 percent having grown nearly four times as fast as the bottom 99 percent.

The increasing share of the top decile is likely a reflection of changes in education, technology, and globalization. The increasing share of the top 1 percent is often attributed to increasingly high-paid managers and CEOs; the incomes of the top 0.1 percent have risen even further, and their income comes mostly from capital income rather than wages. As noted previously, Piketty shows that return on capital is higher than wage-based income or GDP growth and thus contributes to the growth trends in income and wealth shares at the very top.

Income inequality has often been cited by more liberal economists as a detriment to our economy and society, and this position has also been echoed by a major representative of the business sector, Standard & Poor's. Its 2014 report titled *How Increasing Income Inequality Is Dampening U.S. Economic Growth, and Possible Ways to Change the Tide* warned that extreme income inequality can be a drag on long-run economic growth and that the data show our GDP growth in the twenty-first century is about half what it was during the boom period after World War II. Nobel Prize winner Joseph E. Stiglitz concludes in his 2012 book, *The Price of Inequality*, that unequal societies are inefficient and tend to have unstable, unsustainable economies and that income inequality hinders consumption spending and therefore causes a shortfall in consumer demand, which is necessary to sustained growth for all. Henry Ford understood this a century ago when he doubled daily wages to $5 for his auto workers, to both reduce turnover and enable workers to afford the cars they made; both labor and capital were winners.

Piketty says in *Capital in the Twenty-First Century* that capital is winning at the expense of labor in recent decades (note: income earned by US households can be classified as either labor earnings—wages and other forms of compensation—or capital earnings, which includes interest or dividend payments, rent, stock options, and the like). The Federal Reserve Bank of Philadelphia Research Department published a 2015 study concluding that the 2000s witnessed an unprecedented drop in the labor (versus capital) share of income.[32] In the post–World War II period, labor's share of income held pretty steady at around 62 percent of total US income up until about 2000, when it started a steady decline. Confirming the wage stagnation trend, Bureau of Labor Statistics data show that up until the early 1980s, labor productivity and wages grew at a similar rate, but by mid-1985, labor productivity took off, while wage growth was very sluggish. Since then, the gap between productivity and wages has kept growing, depressing the labor share of income. The Federal Reserve study concludes that wage stagnation and the resulting decline of the labor share of total income are a major factor contributing to income inequality because capital is more concentrated across households than labor is. This trend was exacerbated in the recovery from the Great Recession; after 2009, corporate profits, dividend payouts, and the stock market all rose sharply, but wages increased only modestly.

Low-wage jobs in the US are increasing in number as middle-class jobs decline, and these lower-wage workers fare very poorly by international standards, as the OECD's Employment Outlook report shows.[33] In the US, according to the OECD, just over 25 percent of workers had "low-pay" earnings—less than two-thirds of the median wage—which was the highest incidence of low-pay work among the twenty-six countries surveyed and far higher than the OECD average of 16.3 percent. Piketty also speaks to the related issue of social mobility in our society, which he says is lower in the US than in European countries. One factor contributing to lack of social mobility, he suggests, is access to higher education. He cites research showing that the proportion of college degrees in the US earned by children whose parents belong to the bottom two quartiles of the income hierarchy stagnated at 10–20 percent in the 1970–2010 timeframe, while this proportion rose from 40 to 80 percent in the same period for children with parents in the top quartile. He cites college affordability among other advantages of children of wealthy families. So, access to higher education in the US serves as a reinforcing factor in increasing income and wealth inequality.

A 2019 Congressional Budget Office (CBO) updated report on personal income shows a somewhat more positive view on growth in cumulative personal incomes since 1979 (before and after transfers and taxes) than previous reports but still reflects the dramatic growth of the top income groups versus all other income groups, as shown in the accompanying figure for 2016.[34] CBO's results differ from those of other researchers for two principal reasons: (1) CBO includes outlays that employers make for their workers (e.g., payroll taxes and employer contributions toward health insurance and retirement) in addition to cash earnings and income, and (2) CBO uses a different measure of inflation. The increase in income inequality over the thirty-six-year period examined by CBO has been driven primarily by substantial income growth at the top of the income distribution. Federal tax reductions enacted in 2017 are likely to make income inequality worse for future years because the cuts were skewed toward corporations and higher-income earners.

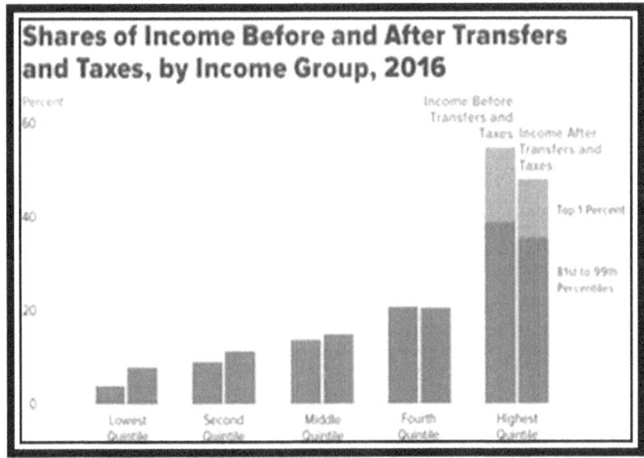

US shares of income by quintile in 2016 (source: Congressional Budget Office)

A 2018 report from OECD makes the case that American policymakers have chosen to design an economic system that leaves US workers disadvantaged, for the sake of directing a higher share of economic growth to bosses and shareholders.[35] It is widely accepted that a degree of income inequality is to be expected in any market economy where economic incentives exist to promote innovation. Steve Jobs, Bill Gates, and other such innovators got rich by inventing technologies that tend to make our lives better. Most people do not begrudge that kind of wealth; on the other hand, financial sector "innovators" created risky investment instruments such as derivatives that helped lead to last decade's economic meltdown, which was detrimental to all segments of society and the economy. In any case, high levels of income inequality in general can be bad for the economy. Keynes and others have shown that income inequality can lead to lower consumption since the wealthy tend to consume a smaller share of their income than poor workers. Those with less means can try to keep up by borrowing to sustain consumption, but this can lead to boom/bust cycles such as the Great Recession. Another argument is that the rich pay higher tax rates to help ensure fairness. Although this is theoretically true at the federal level (the top income tax rate is 39.5 percent as of 2017, but many wealthy individuals pay much less because of lower taxes on capital gains and dividends and use of various tax loopholes), at the state and local levels, the taxes are much more regressive. The Institute on Taxation and Economic Policy calculated that the average overall effective state and local tax rates by income group nationwide are 11.1 percent for the bottom 20 percent, 9.4 percent for the middle 20 percent, and 5.6 percent for the top 1 percent.[36]

In Robert Gordon's comprehensive economic treatise, *The Rise and Fall of American Growth*, he contends that the nation's productivity growth rate, which has already slowed significantly, will be further held back by the headwinds of rising inequality, lack of an adequately educated workforce, an aging population, and the rising debt of college students and the federal government. Gordon warns that the younger generation may be the first in American history to fail to exceed their parents' standard of living. In fact, a study led by Raj Chetty at Stanford, with other researchers at Harvard and Berkeley, estimates that only half the children born in the 1980s earn more than their parents, a drop from 92 percent for children born in the 1940s.[37] This study shows a particularly steep drop for those born in the middle class and for those born in a number of states in the Rust Belt. The researchers attribute a significant portion of this to increasing income inequality, including less upward mobility in a shrinking middle class. Gordon doubts that the incredible improvement in American's standard of living and life expectancy in the last century will be repeated in this century. *New York Times* columnist Russ Douthat, in his book *The Age of Decadence*, suggests that the West in the twenty-first century is one of stalemate and stagnation. He says, "We are aging, comfortable and stuck, cut off from the past and no longer optimistic about the future, spurning both memory and ambition while we await some saving innovation or revelation, growing old unhappily together in the light of tiny screens."

This diminishing economic outlook for less-educated workers was likely a major force that drove the unrest and anger white voters expressed in the 2016 and 2020 presidential election campaigns. It initially caught many establishment politicians, pundits, and policy analysts by surprise, but the discord has persisted. Unfortunately, political soundbites like "Make America Great Again" have little real economic policy substance behind them and resulted in little benefit for left behind Americans. The stock market rebounded strongly from the Great Recession, but that does not help the half of Americans who do not have investment in the market. It is mostly moderate- and low-income Americans who lack access to a retirement account or cannot afford to contribute. There is too little discussion of the economic disparities in our country, and therefore the political solutions offered are often unsuccessful reruns from the last century—for example, "trickle-down" economics.

A very insightful book by Erik Brynjolfsson and Andrew McAfee of MIT—*The Second Machine Age: Work, Progress, and Prosperity in a Time of Brilliant Technologies*—suggests we are in a transformational economic period. The authors suggest that we are in a second industrial-type revolution; this time it is technological, aided by computers, the internet, robotics, and the like. Just like the Industrial Revolution that brought us from an agrarian society to an industrial machine age, the authors contend that we are going through the early phases of a technological revolution, with innovators leading the way and generating high incomes and wealth, which the authors suggest is part of the explanation of growing income and wealth inequality.[38] Jobs for the masses are changing and, in many cases, disappearing in this second machine age.

The McKinsey Global Institute, in its updated December 2017 report *Jobs Lost, Jobs Gained: Workforce Transition in a Time of Automation*, suggests that globally by 2030, 75 million to 375 million workers (3 to 14 percent of the global workforce) will need to switch occupational categories.[39.] Although relatively few job categories are fully susceptible to automation, the report suggests that in 60 percent of occupations, at least one-third of the constituent activities could be automated, implying substantial workplace transformations and changes for all workers. For the United States, the report's midrange estimate suggests that nearly 25 percent of all jobs could be lost to automation. The big question is whether better jobs for these workers will come along in later stages of this economic revolution, as they did with the Industrial Revolution. The various authors are not totally optimistic on this point but say that in any case, we have to prepare a workforce for the twenty-first-century global technological economy. The MIT authors expect that this transformation will take decades to play out and will leave us with a turbulent economic and political generation ahead.

In October 2017, we celebrated the 500th anniversary of the Great Reformation (1517) in Europe; some analysts have drawn parallels between the Reformation (and the Renaissance that helped launch it) and dramatic changes in contemporary society. In their 2017 book *Age of Discovery: Navigating the Risks and Rewards of Our New Renaissance*, Ian Goldin and Chris Kutarna draw comparisons between the turmoil and creativity of the Renaissance of the fifteenth and sixteenth centuries (and the Reformation that it spurred) and the dramatic changes that we are experiencing in our twenty-first-century world. They suggest, for example, that the invention of the printing press was to the Renaissance and Reformation what the internet is to us today. The internet, effectively nonexistent twenty years ago, linked one billion people by 2005, two billion people by 2010, and three billion people by 2015. Now more than half of humanity is online! Human health, wealth, and education are better for millions, and scientific discovery is delivering unprecedented achievements for the betterment of society. Many suggest that this is the best moment in history to be alive. But the same global flows of trade, capital, people, and ideas that make gains possible for many also deliver losses to others. This is leading to religious, cultural, and political turmoil in the United States and many other parts of the world. This is reminiscent of the first Renaissance and Reformation, which democratized communication and sparked a flourishing of creative achievement (led by the likes of Columbus, Copernicus, Gutenberg, and Luther), but during which time the world also grappled with a similar dark side of rapid change leading to social division and political extremism. As then, now we are in a contest between the bright and dark sides of rapid discovery; we can flourish and exceed the first if we learn lessons of the past and get our incentives right.

Reid Hoffman, the founder of LinkedIn, argues that it is not only companies that must harness new technologies to thrive in a competitive world; people must harness them as well. He says, "Competition is fierce. The world is changing. And the amount of time you spend at any one job is shrinking. This means you need to be adapting all the time. And if you fail to adapt, no one—not your employer, not the government—is going to catch you when you fall." Some argue for a permanent income floor for American workers, but that idea faces significant political opposition. On the other hand, there is already some bipartisan support for expanding earned income tax credits (EITC), which would have a similar effect to help provide life-sustaining incomes for lower-income working families. A wage supplement for lower-paying jobs is another recent proposed alternative; it is similar to the EITC, but it would boost hourly pay directly rather than require low-income workers to wait for a one-time supplement after tax returns are filed. Unfortunately, it is only too clear that our current political system is ill-prepared to guide us forward in these uncertain times. We can only hope that the policy debate will improve as we achieve greater understanding of these unprecedented twenty-first century economic forces.

In the first major written work of his papacy, Pope Francis attacked unfettered capitalism as "a new tyranny," urging global leaders to fight poverty and growing inequality. The eighty-four-page document, known as an apostolic exhortation, is essentially an official platform for his papacy.[40] In it, Pope Francis went further than in previous comments attacking the "idolatry of money" and beseeching politicians to guarantee all citizens "dignified work, education and healthcare." Francis wrote, "It is the consequence of a global choice, an economic system which leads to this tragedy; an economic system which has at its centre an idol called money ... How can it be that it is not a news item when an elderly homeless person dies of exposure, but it is news when the stock market loses two points?"

Unfortunately, with the Trump administration we saw a lot of backward-looking economic proposals related to trade and tariffs to try to bring back old manufacturing jobs. Manufacturing employment has declined in America over the past few decades, but the major reason is automation, not trade. And automation has contributed to increased manufacturing output. A study by Michael J. Hicks and Srikant Devaraj at Ball State University showed that manufacturing has experienced good growth in the United States.[41] The authors show that despite the recessionary period, manufacturing output grew by 17.6 percent, or about 2.2 percent a year, from 2006 to 2013. But unfortunately, the decade from 2000 to 2010 saw "the largest decline in manufacturing employment in U.S. history," per the Ball State study. What killed those jobs for the most part was not global trade, but productivity gains from automation. The report notes that over this decade, productivity gains accounted for some 87 percent of lost manufacturing jobs, while trade was responsible for just 13 percent. And unfortunately, there could be more manufacturing job loss on the horizon. The CEO of Dynamic (a maker of molds for the mass production of small plastic and metal parts), Joe McGillivray, describes a vision of a manufacturing system that transforms raw materials into finished products without human labor— "one touch manufacturing," he calls it.

Despite the automation trends, the Manufacturing

Institute says there are skilled manufacturing jobs available but also shortages of workers with adequate tech skills. Some good examples of community colleges filling this retraining vacuum are beginning to emerge. By collaborating with local manufacturing companies, community colleges have shown a possible model for meeting this growing need of "smart" manufacturing jobs. Great Bay Community College in Rochester, New Hampshire, is one example, where the collaborators are focusing on "composite" manufacturing—that is, blending fiber materials for high-strength alternatives to metal. The American Enterprise Institute presented three case studies of community colleges partnering with the automotive industry to help get students job ready. Two of the three partnerships—Mercedes-Benz with Shelton State Community College and Volkswagen with Chattanooga State Community College—place students on a clear pathway from college to employment at the partner's factory. In contrast, a third program—one between State University of New York (SUNY) Canton and Subaru—approaches the partnership as a mutually beneficial opportunity to leverage shared resources and, in the process, help students gain valuable workplace skills. Subaru helps SUNY Canton outfit on-campus lab space, and the community college agrees to share the lab space with Subaru for new employee training. This is where the focus should be regarding manufacturing, not on promises to bring back old manufacturing jobs from abroad. We should be embracing improved productivity and offering job retraining programs for the technological revolution that is emerging, not fighting it. For the future, there should be more vocational training opportunities beginning in high school that are oriented to today's industry needs. Many industry jobs, although more technical than in the past, do not necessarily require a college degree.

An important topic regarding economic inequality is the influence of money in our electoral process. The influence of Super PACs (i.e., political action committees), undisclosed donations, and online political campaigning, including foreign intervention, have emerged as potential threats to our democracy. Our campaign finance system was largely formed through the Federal Election Campaign Act Amendments of 1973, which envisioned a comprehensive set of restrictions on contributions and expenditures, from all identifiable sources of money in the system. The current system of campaign finance is dramatically different from the system envisioned in the 1970s, through both law changes and court decisions. The Bipartisan Campaign Reform Act of 2002, also known as "McCain-Feingold," after its sponsors, was the most recent major federal law change on campaign finance. It prohibited unregulated contributions (so-called soft money) to national political parties and limited the use of corporate and union money to fund ads discussing political issues within sixty days of a general election or thirty days of a primary election. However, it was struck down by the Supreme Court in 2010 on constitutional grounds in *Citizens United vs. Federal Election Commission*. Super PACs specifically were enabled with the DC Circuit's decision in *SpeechNOW.org v. FEC* (2010), which permitted them to accept contributions in unlimited amounts for their independent spending.

These and other campaign finance changes since the 1973 law have produced a system in which all significant players can spend unlimited amounts on campaign-related expenditures and often without disclosure. And now digital campaigning has rapidly emerged and is conducive to undisclosed political spending, including foreign intervention. Since the web is worldwide, foreign influence is much easier than it once was, as we saw with Russian influence in the 2016 presidential election.

Virtually all changes to campaign finance have benefited the wealthy at the expense of those of moderate income, so this is another rapidly emerging area of economic inequality in the nation. Donors who can provide large contributions are likely to have disproportionate influence over public policy, protecting their own economic or other interests regardless of what is good for the broader public. Perhaps most disturbing is the daily influence of big money on Capitol Hill; congressional representatives are reported to spend upward of 70 percent of their time on fundraising, and this mostly focuses on chasing the big donors, who of course expect something in return!

The term 'inclusive capitalism' has emerged internationally over the last decade; it seeks to make our economic system more equitable, sustainable, and inclusive. The idea is that nations need to ensure both that economic growth takes place, and that this growth is broadly shared with its citizens. Advocates also suggest that nations succeed when their citizens are secure in the expectation that those willing to work will be able to work and that standards of living will increase. Without that expectation, citizens lose confidence in their institutions, social cohesion suffers, confidence in the future erodes, and resistance builds. These ideas are articulated in the *Report of the Commission on Inclusive Prosperity* headed by Larry Summers, a former Clinton and Obama economic adviser, and Ed Balls, a top British Labor Party politician.[42] The report focuses on new economic, social, and political approaches to make twenty-first-century capitalism work for the many. A key concern of such advocates in the US is that labor's share of the economy continues to decline. Although the economy is improving, wages are relatively stagnant, and many emerging jobs are in lower-paying sectors (e.g., retail, fast food), leading to labor's relative decline as compared to capital.

Advocates of inclusive capitalism say that both major

political parties must be more flexible in addressing our nation's economic problems. They suggest that although some extremes on both the political left and right seek to turn away from globalization and technological advancement, such withdrawal is not a realistic option for our nation as we compete in an increasingly worldwide market. Businesses that do not adapt to new technology inevitably lose out in global competition. Advocates embrace the need for successful entrepreneurs and wealth creation to finance new investment to achieve economic progress, but at the same time they emphasize that labor must benefit as well if we are to have a successful economy. They also reject a return to laissez-faire, trickle-down economics that includes cutting taxes at the top, eliminating regulation, and making deep cuts to safety-net programs because this will only lead to a nation that is more and more unequal.

Advocates of inclusive capitalism imagine creating a more inclusive economy with good jobs, decent salaries, and a hopeful future for all its citizens. They see this as possible but believe that it will require a concerted effort and a major shift in policy across a number of areas. They say that powerful forces of globalization and technological change must be navigated, or inequalities will continue to widen, and for many, low-skill work will increasingly become the norm. Proposals for inclusive capitalism embrace changes such as major revisions of the tax code, legislation to pressure or provide incentives for corporations to increase pay to match productivity growth, expansion of EITC for lower-income workers, and other possible wage-supplement approaches. Education is a major theme of inclusive capitalism, which stresses continuous investment in our citizens, from cradle to sustainable economic livelihoods. The US lags other industrialized countries in preschool education and is falling behind in higher-education access and job-readiness training.

A similar movement, conscious capitalism, was inspired by John Mackey, Whole Foods cofounder and co-CEO, and Raj Sisodia, professor of marketing at Bentley University, through their book *Conscious Capitalism: Liberating the Heroic Spirit of Business*. Their credo acknowledges that while free-market capitalism is the most powerful system for social cooperation and human progress, people can aspire to achieve more. This movement resulted in an organization called Conscious Capitalism Inc. that builds on the core foundations of capitalism—voluntary exchange, entrepreneurship, competition, freedom to trade, and the rule of law. The credo adds elements like trust, compassion, collaboration, and value creation.

Finally, a movement known as the triple bottom line (TBL) evolved over the last two decades. This concept recommends that companies commit to focusing on social and environmental concerns just as they do on profits. The TBL posits that instead of one bottom line, there should be three: profit, people, and the planet. A TBL seeks to gauge a corporation's level of commitment to corporate social responsibility and its impact on the environment over time. Green movements worldwide have been particular advocates of this concept. Companies are increasingly being challenged to have more sustainable supply chains and production processes. An additional factor forcing companies to look again at their extended supply chains to China and other such far-flung markets is the recent threat of pandemic viruses.

As mentioned earlier, Germany is often seen as a model for the way in which it supports and networks with employers to train workers in apprenticeships following secondary school education. Without these types of initiatives, advocates of inclusive capitalism suggest that our society will continue to become more unequal, and more families will fall into poverty and lose hope for the future. A study by Harvard researchers called *Pathways to Prosperity* suggests the need for a revival of vocational education in secondary schools to help stem the higher high school drop-out rates for boys, a pattern that occurs in every single state. The study cites several existing programs that could serve as a model for national reform, including the Massachusetts system, sometimes called the Cadillac of career training education. Massachusetts has a network of twenty-six academically rigorous vocational-technical high schools serving 27,000 students. Students in magnet schools with vocational emphases take traditional academic courses but spend half their time apprenticing in a field of their choice. These fields include computer repair, telecommunications networking, carpentry, early childhood education, plumbing, heating, refrigeration, and cosmetology. These schools have some of the state's highest graduation and college matriculation rates. Community colleges collaborating with local industry are also effective, as noted earlier—the American Enterprise Institute highlights successful auto industry examples such as Mercedes-Benz working with Shelton State Community College and Volkswagen with Chattanooga State Community College to place students on a clear pathway from college to employment at their factories.

In his 2013 State of the Union, President Obama said, "Let's declare that in the wealthiest nation on earth, no one who works full-time should have to live in poverty." This position is consistent with the idea of a living wage. "Living wage" is a term used to describe the minimum hourly wage necessary for an individual to meet basic needs, including shelter (housing), food, medical needs, clothing, transportation, and the like. The need for such a wage is why many are pushing for a higher minimum wage nationwide, and the effort has been led by metropolitan areas across the country that have pushed well beyond the federal minimum. As mentioned earlier, the EITC is also a mechanism for underpinning a basic living wage, and there seems to be bipartisan support for expanding it. We also need greater investment in R&D and infrastructure to help make our nation more competitive.

William Galston of the Brookings Institution suggests that America must restore the norm of gainful employment for all who are mentally and physically able and are not working in the home and that both the public and the private sector must share responsibility for equipping every American, college-bound or not, with skills relevant to the twenty-first-century market and that are sustainable through inevitable downturns. This strategy must include addressing the increasing geographic divide in economic growth between major metropolitan areas and rural and small communities.

4

Poverty and Homelessness

Homelessness is the most visible inequity of poverty that keeps not only housing but also many other basic resources out of reach for millions of Americans, including adequate education, health care, employment, adequate income, and safe and healthy neighborhoods. These longstanding inequities and intergenerational poverty are the troubling result of not only economic inequality but also a history of discrimination in employment, housing, incarceration, and many other aspects of life.

The growing gap between wage earnings and the cost of housing in the United States leaves millions of families and individuals unable to make ends meet. A surprising number of people work at low-wage jobs. Social Security wage data, which includes both full- and part-time workers, shows that just under half of all American wage earners make less than $30,000 annually, barely above the poverty level for a family of four.[43] As noted earlier, analysis suggests that a full-time worker earning the federal minimum wage of $7.25 per hour cannot rent an affordable two-bedroom apartment anywhere in the country, according to the National Low-Income Housing Coalition. Further, such low-income individuals and families living on the margins are vulnerable to unexpected crises, like the recent coronavirus pandemic which can lead to homelessness.

A great divide separates affluent Americans from the growing portion of the population whose lives lack stability or any real prospect of betterment. It was recently reported that a hedge-fund billionaire had paid $238 million for a New York apartment overlooking Central Park, which he plans to use only when he happens to be in town! Meanwhile, millions of American families can barely afford an apartment. They often spend more than half of their income on rent and have to scrimp on food and health care. This vulnerability has been dramatically increased during COVID-19 as increasing numbers are unable to make rent payments. On any given night, more than half a million Americans are homeless and this number is rising as a result of the pandemic.

Poverty Trends

For the US, the Census Bureau reported the official poverty rate in 2019 was 10.5 percent, down from 11.8 percent in 2018.[44] Despite the improvement, though, poverty remains deeply entrenched, particularly among African Americans and Hispanics. Before the pandemic of 2020, there were about 34 million people living in poverty in the United States, including some 12 million children, with higher percentages among minority families. Children suffer many disadvantages living in poverty, including those involving health and nutrition, educational opportunity, and future life prospects. With the economy tanking during the coronavirus, millions more have likely fallen into poverty. During one week in late July 2020 nearly 30 million Americans reported they did not have enough to eat, according to a government survey. Among households with children, one in three reported insufficient food, the highest level in the nearly two decades the government has tracked hunger in America, said Lauren Bauer, who studies food insecurity at the Brookings Institution.

I was privileged to hear Dr. Raphael Warnock, pastor of the historic Ebenezer Baptist Church in Atlanta (and now a Georgia Senator), where Dr. Martin Luther King Jr. served with his father, speak here in DC in June 2018. He talked about the legacy of Dr. King and the still "unfinished business" around racism and poverty. He reminded us that King died in service to poor workers—sanitation workers. One of the startling reminders that Warnock emphasized was that in America we punish the poor; poverty is too often treated as a crime. Mass incarceration has been a favorite tool for decades to hide the problem. Few politicians ever utter the word "poor" or acknowledge the poor among their constituents. Dr. Warnock suggested that when the poor are mentioned by politicians, it is often in a negative context, via terms such as "takers," "welfare cheats," "criminals," and the like.

A United Nations (UN) study released in June 2018, *Report of the Special Rapporteur on Extreme Poverty and Human Rights on His Mission to the United States of America*, highlights that just under 40 million Americans live in poverty, and 18.5 million live in "extreme poverty."[45] The UN report also notes that a high number of children were living in poverty in 2016—about 13.3 million, or 18 percent—with government spending on children near the bottom in international comparisons and that the poverty rates are much higher for minorities. The Brookings Institution's Hamilton Project on poverty notes,

> For children, poverty means living with the stress that comes from insufficient nutritional intake, living in the presence of violence in their community or household, and not having a secure

place to sleep at night. These challenges make it harder for children to learn and thrive in school, which, in turn, leads to problems that cumulate over childhood and into adulthood. The concern is that children born into deprivation will live their lives stuck in a perpetual poverty trap.

The aforementioned UN report further notes that the United States has the highest rate of income inequality among Western countries. It reports that in 1981, the top 1 percent of adults earned on average twenty-seven times more than the bottom 50 percent of adults. Today the top 1 percent earn eighty-one times more than the bottom 50 percent, and the United States in 2018 had over 25 percent of the world's billionaires. The report also highlights that almost a quarter of full-time workers and three-quarters of part-time workers in the US receive no paid sick leave. Absence from work due to illness thus poses a risk of economic disaster. About 44 percent of adults either could not cover an emergency expense costing $400 or would need to sell something or borrow money to do it. Yet the report notes that our policies seem to only exacerbate the situations of poverty and income inequality; they are often designed to remove basic protections from the poorest and punish those who are not employed, and they fail to extend basic health care to all while tax cuts are tilted to the wealthy and corporations.

The UN report concludes with these observations and recommendations:

- Punishing and imprisoning the poor is the distinctively American response to poverty in the twenty-first century. Workers who cannot pay their debts, those who cannot afford private probation services, minorities targeted for traffic infractions, the homeless, the mentally ill, fathers who cannot pay child support and many others are all locked up. Mass incarceration is used to make social problems temporarily invisible and to create the mirage of something having been done.

- It is difficult to imagine a more self-defeating strategy. Federal, state, county and city governments incur vast costs in running jails and prisons. Sometimes these costs are "recovered" from the prisoners, thus fueling the latter's cycle of poverty and desperation. The criminal records attached to the poor through imprisonment make it even harder for them to find jobs, housing, stability, and self-sufficiency. Families are destroyed, children are left parentless and the burden on governments mounts. But because little is done to address the underlying causes of the original problem, it continues to fester. Even when imprisonment is not the preferred option, the standard response to those facing economic hardship is to adopt policies explicitly designed to make access to health care, sick leave and welfare and child benefits more difficult to access and the receipt of benefits more stigmatizing.

- A cheaper and more humane option is to provide proper social protection and facilitate the return to the workforce of those who are able. In the United States, it is poverty that needs to be arrested, not the poor simply for being poor.

The availability of full-time jobs at a decent wage is essential for people to move out of poverty, but it is not necessarily enough. Many poor people, stuck with a deficient education, inadequate health care, and limited work skills, find that small setbacks can quickly set off a downward spiral. Geographic and intergenerational poverty are particularly challenging phenomena. The Equality of Opportunity Project of Harvard University has released studies concluding that children growing up in poor neighborhoods anywhere are at a lifetime disadvantage, and the project specifically found for Baltimore that the income mobility for poor children there is worse than in any large county in America.[46] The Harvard researchers, Raj Chetty and Nathaniel Hendren, write that every additional year spent in inner-city Baltimore "reduces a child's earnings by 0.7 percent per year, generating a total earnings penalty of approximately 14 percent for children who grow up there from birth." The Harvard studies show that poor kids who left poor neighborhoods were much more likely to go to college and earn more. Chetty estimates that giving families with kids (age eight on average) a voucher to move into low-poverty areas increases the child's lifetime earnings by about $302,000. The data also suggest that girls of such families are 26 percent less likely to become single mothers. In a larger study, Chetty and other colleagues looked at earnings data for five million families in the US over seventeen years. The findings were the same: neighborhoods matter for children.

Economist Justin Wolfers writes that these studies "are the most powerful demonstration yet that neighborhoods—their schools, community, neighbors, local amenities, economic opportunities, and social norms—are a critical factor shaping your children's outcomes." Several factors are likely in play here. Many social scientists suggest that peers are more important than parents in determining how kids turn out. Others argue that parents, particularly married parents, are the crucial factor. And everyone agrees that schools, criminal justice policies, and racial attitudes are important variables. Regardless of the relative importance of each factor, in extremely poor neighborhoods these factors combine to disadvantage children growing up in those poor communities. In middle-class neighborhoods, these factors seem to reinforce each other in positive ways. This new work builds on findings of a 2011 *American Sociological Review* article by sociologists Geoffrey Wodtke and David Hardi, which found that growing up in a poor neighborhood significantly reduced the chances that a child would graduate from high school, and the longer a child lived in that kind of neighborhood, the more harmful the impact.[47]

Researchers at Brandeis University recently analyzed census tract data to understand how a child's neighborhood influences his or her opportunities over time. They found strong racial and ethnic divides regarding opportunity. Neighborhoods were rated and assigned an "opportunity level" ranging from "very low" to "very high" on such factors as access to early childhood education, high school graduation rates, the share of adults in high-skill jobs, poverty rates, air pollution levels, and housing vacancy rates. The researchers found that across the nation's largest metro areas, 46 percent of Black children and 32 percent of Hispanic children live in "very low" opportunity neighborhoods, and Black children are 7.6 times and Hispanic children 5.3 times more likely than white children to live in very low-opportunity neighborhoods.

Another disturbing finding of research on the impact of living in poor neighborhoods is that the negative effects extend across generations. An article on intergenerational poverty published in 2009, titled "The Long-Term Consequences of Growing Up Poor," by Robert Lee Wagmiller and Robert M. Adelman, shows that adults who were poor during childhood are much more likely to be poor in early and middle adulthood than are those who were never poor, and the trend is much more pronounced among African Americans.[48]

Given that poverty is a serious intergenerational problem, solutions must be comprehensive. Children of poor families once housed, need additional intervention, particularly in educational resources (starting with access to pre-K) to help the next generation escape the effects of poverty. Health access and adequate food and nutrition are other important factors for such families. And of course, the importance of good jobs for household heads cannot be overstated. This suggests the importance of local communities linking programs in areas such as housing, job training, child education, health, and nutrition rather than taking traditional silo approaches.

Homelessness—National and DC Trends and Experience

Homelessness rose 2.7 percent from 2018 to 2019, according to the annual assessment by the Department of Housing and Urban Development (HUD) published just before the COVID-19 pandemic.[49] A 16.4 percent increase in homelessness in California was a significant contributor to the increase. HUD highlighted the homelessness problem in California, finding that more than a quarter of the nation's homeless population reside in the state, totaling about 151,000 people out of a US total of 567,715 estimated homeless each night in 2019. Although the Centers for Disease Control (CDC) estimates that 1.7 percent of the US population currently experiences homelessness, it says that with over 34 million people living in poverty and another 19 million experiencing housing insecurity, over 10 percent of the total population is potentially at risk for homelessness at any given time. Still, twenty-nine states and the District of Columbia reported declines in the number of people living on the streets. There were also pockets of progress nationally, as veteran homelessness went down 2.1 percent, homelessness among families with children decreased 4.8 percent, and the number of homeless youth and children went down 3.6 percent, HUD reported.

The National Alliance to End Homelessness highlights that homelessness and poverty are inextricably linked. Poor people are frequently unable to pay the full costs of housing, food, childcare, health care, and education. Difficult choices must be made when limited resources cover only some of these necessities. Often it is housing, which absorbs a high proportion of income, that must be dropped. If you are poor, you are essentially an illness, an accident, or a paycheck away from living on the streets. The Alliance expects the pandemic to exacerbate housing vulnerability as eviction protections and other temporary benefits expire.

Homelessness in America has multiple causes and correlations. Chronic health conditions and disabling conditions are both a cause and a consequence of homelessness. Experts stress that among people who experience homelessness, age fifty from a chronological perspective is more like age seventy-five in terms of health and geriatric conditions. Chronic stress and trauma are pervasive among the homeless population and escape from and further exposure to victimization are a special concern for women experiencing homelessness. Other notable risk correlations among the homeless population include being LGBTQ, having a history of institutionalization, and having a behavioral health condition.

However, most telling among all the statistics is the racial disparity embedded within the risk factors cited previously.

Race plays an outsized role in the profile of homelessness in America, with Black Americans making up about 40 percent of those who experience homelessness but only 13 percent of the overall population. In DC, African Americans make up 47 percent of the general population but 87 percent of adults experiencing homelessness. This truth exposes intergenerational race-based disenfranchisement in housing, education, jobs, and other services that have been a part of our nation's history. To quote Ta-Nehisi Coates[50]:

> If you sought to advantage one group of Americans and disadvantage another, you could scarcely choose a more graceful method than housing discrimination. Housing determines access to transportation, green spaces, decent schools, decent food, decent jobs, and decent services. Housing affects your chances of being robbed and shot as well as your chances of being stopped and frisked. Housing discrimination is hard to detect, hard to prove, and hard to prosecute.

Over the past century, Coates and others suggest, federal and local housing policies along with neighborhood decisions and behavior have overtly and covertly segregated and impoverished the Black population through practices such as redlining, race-based housing covenants, and limitations on government-backed mortgages and other lending. Exclusion from housing opportunity and displacement from their homes not only segregated the Black community but also prevented it from participating in wealth accumulation, thereby setting off the compounding damages of intergenerational poverty. Though the 1968 Fair Housing Act outlawed many of these racist policies, it did not do so in time to prevent extreme privation and injury to the Black/African American community. Price appreciation and exclusion from the housing market had already created highly segregated communities and the wealth gap between white and Black neighborhoods. Sadly, the Trump Administration, as a blatant campaign appeal to suburban voters, repealed a fair housing rule that the President claimed would lead to "destruction" of the country's suburbs. The Affirmatively Furthering Fair Housing rule being eliminated was proposed by President Obama in 2015 to combat housing discrimination and segregation by requiring cities and towns to scrutinize their housing patterns for racial bias and address solutions.

5

Case Study on Ending Long-Term Homelessness in the Nation's Capital

Our nation's capital, Washington, DC, part of the wealthiest metropolitan area in the nation, has one of the highest rates of poverty and homelessness in the country. In addition to some 6,500 singles and family members who experience homelessness every night in the District, thousands more are living in doubled-up, crowded, and unstable situations.

Washington, DC statistics regarding homelessness both mirror and exaggerate the national data. DC has long been highly segregated by income and race and remains so to this day. Until 2011, DC was a majority-Black city. Over the past two decades, DC has seen enormous population growth, with in-migration of wealthier white residents displacing many lower-income Black families. Despite recent efforts to help alleviate the problem through tools such as inclusionary zoning, rental subsidies, and developer incentives, the District has lost over half of its affordable housing stock in the past decade, with a disproportionate impact on Black residents.

The District's Interagency Council on Homelessness (ICH) was established by the Homeless Services Reform Act of 2005 for the purpose of facilitating interagency coordination with regard to planning, policymaking, program development, and budgeting for the homeless services system in the District, and the ICH is required to develop a new strategic plan every five years. However, it was not staffed until several years after its creation. There are now three full-time positions that staff the ICH, led by executive director Kristy Greenwalt. The staffing has been a significant asset to the ICH's effectiveness in planning and executing plans for addressing DC's homelessness challenge.

Given the increasing homeless population in DC overall, including singles and families and among them veterans, the ICH developed a bold five-year (2015–20) strategic plan— "Homeward DC"—to end long-term homelessness in the District by 2020. Specifically, Homeward DC proposed to "1) Finish the job of ending homelessness among Veterans by the end of 2015, 2) End chronic homelessness among individuals and families by 2017, and 3) Assure by 2020 that homelessness in D.C. will be a rare, brief, and non-recurring experience." The city's mayor, Muriel Bowser, strongly committed to the plan, which was released shortly after she came into office in 2015. She said in her plan release letter, "The District has higher rates of chronic homelessness than other similarly sized cities in America, and family homelessness has increased a staggering 50 percent over the past five years … When I entered office on January 2, the District's homeless crisis was at the top of my priority list." Under the plan over the last five years, there have been major investments in both reforming the homeless services system and increasing the supply of affordable housing through the DC Housing Production Trust Fund, the Housing Preservation Fund, and other policy tools, but as will be discussed later, the challenges of homelessness have been larger than the resources available.

Homeward DC highlighted the challenge facing the city: "Homelessness and poverty are inextricably linked. Poor people are frequently unable to pay for housing, food, childcare, health care, and education … If you are poor, you are essentially an illness, an accident, or a paycheck away from living on the streets." Stable housing is out of reach for many DC residents, many of whom have lived in the District their entire lives and are finding themselves priced out of a rapidly gentrifying urban market. DC is one of the most expensive rental markets in the country, with the median rental cost for a single-bedroom apartment reported at over $2,000 per month. Because of this situation, it has become increasingly difficult for people to quickly exit shelter back to permanent housing.

In May 2016, the city council unanimously approved a plan to close the city's dilapidated homeless shelter for families at DC General Hospital and replace it with a network of seven smaller family shelters referred to as short-term family housing (STFH), to be constructed in neighborhoods across the city, each in a different ward. All wards except Ward 2 would have a new STFH family shelter; Ward 2 was selected for the new Pat Handy shelter for women, which is operated by N Street Village (see subsequent discussion about the Village, of which I am a board member). Despite months of back-and-forth between the mayor and the council over details of the seven wards' family shelters and continued criticism from residents, DC officials were eventually able to move ahead with the project, which is estimated to cost almost a half billion dollars over twenty-five years. The STFH projects were gradually opened over subsequent years with completion to be accomplished by the end of 2020.

Each year in January, DC and other cities conduct a point-in-time (PIT) survey of homeless populations. The DC Community Partnership for the Prevention of Homelessness leads the survey. The 2020 PIT results showed that the total number of persons experiencing homelessness in the District decreased by 2.2 percent from 6,521 to 6,380 persons. Family homelessness decreased by 5.8 percent since the 2019 PIT and by 48.5 percent since the 2016 PIT count. The number of individuals experiencing homelessness however has continued to increase modestly each year with a 1.9 percent in the last year. On the positive side, there was a continued decrease in the number of individuals experiencing chronic homelessness, dropping from 1,501 in 2016 to 1,337 in 2020. The 2020 PIT shows that of the 6380 persons experiencing homelessness, there were:

- 653 unsheltered persons (i.e., persons "on the street"),
- 4,526 persons in Emergency Shelters, and
- 1,201 persons in Transitional Housing facilities.

In 2019, the ICH reviewed its first three fiscal years of progress on Homeward DC and published a report titled *Homeward DC Performance Report.*[51] As mentioned earlier, the Homeward DC plan (1.0) was developed by the ICH in 2015 to guide the District's efforts at reforming its homeless services system, with the ultimate goal of ending chronic homeless and ensuring homelessness in the District is rare, brief, and nonrecurring. The assessment highlights that approximately 60,000 households in the District are severely rent-burdened, and any shock to the household (job loss, reduction in hours, a health crisis, a death, or divorce) can lead to housing loss and homelessness.

The ICH review also shows that results for families experiencing homelessness are moving in positive directions, helped by the initiatives made under the Homeward DC strategic plan. The city made significant investments in homelessness prevention assistance (to stabilize families at risk of homelessness) and permanent housing assistance (to help families experiencing a housing crisis return to housing of their own). Following the launch of the Homeward DC plan in 2015, family homelessness was reduced from 1,491 households in January 2016 to 767 in the January 2020 PIT. The city has been able to offer a housing resource for every family entering the homeless services system, which has made a big impact on the ability to reduce family homelessness. As mentioned earlier, one of the biggest investments in time and resources over the past four years has been the reforms in the shelter system for families, with replacement of the old DC General shelter with smaller STFH sites throughout the city.

The assessment of the situation in the system for single adults is less positive. The number of single adults in the homeless services system each year increased from 3683 in January 2016 to 3947 in January 2020. Because of the significant investment in overhauling the family system, there have been fewer resources to devote to singles. Also, the single-adult homeless population is older and more vulnerable than originally assumed; they are not self-resolving at the rate assumed, and many more need permanent supportive housing (PSH) than assumed in the original plan. As a result, the city has been able to offer permanent housing for only about one in ten single homeless persons entering the system. Looking to the next five years for Homeward DC (2.0), it's likely that most all single individuals experiencing chronic homelessness will need PSH, presenting a significant challenge for the city and its providers in capacity and resources going forward (note: an individual is considered chronically homeless when he or she (1) resides in a shelter or place not meant for human habitation, (2) has a disabling condition, and (3) has been homeless continuously for a year or more or has had at least four separate episodes of homelessness within a three-year period). One final note regarding singles is that the District has made progress in reducing homelessness among veterans, for whom significant new housing resources were appropriated during the Obama administration. Between 2014 and 2018, the District reduced homelessness among veterans by 25 percent although there was a slight increase in the 2020 PIT.

Regarding single adult homeless women (who constitute about 25 percent of the single homeless population in DC), survey data showed the following:

- Single women are an older demographic (averaging fifty-two) and are disproportionately African American.
- About one-third of women indicate that violence is the cause of their homelessness or housing instability.
- Mental illness and substance abuse are primary challenges for women, and much of this is trauma related.
- Their age and disabilities make employment particularly challenging.

Further, a 2017 ICH Women's Needs Assessment found that over half (56 percent) of women experiencing homelessness are survivors of domestic or intimate partner violence, and half had experiences of violence perpetrated by a parent or guardian. This is the population served at N Street Village, now the largest provider of services in DC, which will be discussed later in this chapter.

One of the most important developments in the system for single adults in recent years is the development of the District's Coordinated Assessment and Housing Placement system. This system has increased the District's ability to identify and reach vulnerable individuals; it allows more efficiency in matching the right resource to the right client; and it has increased understanding of the single homeless population, resulting in a more challenging picture than realized at the time the Homeward DC 1.0 plan was issued in 2015. The city review says:

> While all low-income households would benefit from rental assistance or access to an affordable unit, providing everyone that touches the homeless services system with a subsidy or permanent affordable housing has not proven feasible. The initial Homeward DC plan assumed that the city would provide the lightest touch intervention needed to resolve each person's homelessness, targeting the most intensive resources to those households with the most intensive needs. The plan also assumed that the District would continue to invest in affordable housing; and although significant investments have been made in permanent housing, the demand has continued to outstrip the supply.

As background before we look ahead, it should be noted that there are three types of housing programs currently used in the DC homeless services system:

- Rapid Re-Housing (RRH): time-limited rental assistance and case management support to help individuals and families with less intensive service needs return to permanent housing. This resource needs to be paired with employment supports to be successful.

- Targeted Affordable Housing (TAH): deep, ongoing rental assistance with light-touch case management support to help households with fixed incomes but less intensive supportive service needs. This resource is often targeted to seniors and persons with physical disabilities who do not need ongoing case management support to maintain their housing.
- Permanent Supportive Housing (PSH): deep, ongoing rental assistance with intensive, ongoing case management support. This resource is targeted to the most vulnerable individuals who often have behavioral health conditions in addition to physical disabilities and/or chronic health conditions.

In recent years, the United States Interagency Council on Homelessness and HUD have identified RRH as a critical strategy for meeting the national goal of ending family homelessness by 2020. RRH is an intervention that helps homeless families or individuals exit shelters or transitional housing and get back into permanent housing as quickly as possible. It also provides short-term help with housing expenses (e.g., rent assistance, moving costs) and case management to support housing stability. But the National Alliance to End Homelessness estimates that there are only about one-third of the needed housing placements for families experiencing homelessness each year. DC has adopted RRH as the primary tool for securing permanent housing for homeless families, but for the single-adult homeless population, RRH has been less successful. In the case of chronically homeless individuals, most will need PSH.

For single adults, significant investments were focused on PSH over the last five-year period, including nearly 2,300 new units of PSH. With these investments, over 4,800 individuals exited the streets or shelters to permanent housing, including hundreds of individuals with long histories of homelessness. However, there has been approximately a 20 percent annual increase in adults entering the District's homeless services since the plan was released in 2015. So, despite the large investments in PSH in recent years, a significant shortfall remains. This means that the city had individuals entering homelessness in recent years faster than they exit, resulting in an increase in homelessness for individuals as noted in the annual PIT results. Further, with the increased new inflow of individuals into the homeless services system each year and a lack of resources or capacity to immediately assist people in the system, more will transition into chronic status.

The city invested more heavily in tenant-based subsidies to increase PSH than in project-based subsidies tied to new construction of affordable units. The tenant-based vouchers allowed the District to move more quickly to offer housing opportunity, but experience shows it took clients an exceptionally long time to locate units. Clients with poor credit or rental history, as well as clients with any sort of criminal history, faced especially steep barriers. The other challenge faced is the more rapid increase in rental costs than anticipated in the plan, so for any given budget fewer households were served than anticipated. It is clear the District needs more construction of affordable housing stock, including PSH, so that will be a focus of the next five years.

Another important measure of performance is the number of returns to homelessness. The review shows positively that District results are consistent with national averages for both families and individuals (approximately 15 percent) and have remained consistent over the last few years. Length of stay in shelter was also reviewed, and mixed results were found, with singles showing somewhat shorter stays over the period and families incurring longer stays, although there were data challenges particularly with singles, where there tends to be sporadic use of the homeless services system.

With an extensive analysis of inflow patterns to the homeless services system completed by the Community Partnership in 2018, it is now believed that the number of individuals experiencing chronic homelessness in the District throughout the course of the year is much higher than thought, in the range of 4,000. In addition to the 1,374 chronically homeless individuals identified on the night of the PIT, the estimate also includes people experiencing chronic homelessness but not counted in the city's system the night of the PIT and people expected to evolve into chronic status during the year.

At a 2019 Greater Washington Community Foundation event in DC focusing on the housing crisis, Schroeder Stribling, CEO of N Street Village, said, "The rate we transition people out of shelter is not keeping up with the rate of people coming into the shelter. We will not charity our way out of this problem … it is going to take all of us working together." Scott Schenkelberg, CEO of Miriam's Kitchen, said at the same forum that "it costs $40,000 per year to keep someone homeless in DC. Permanent Supportive Housing (PSH) is more cost effective—it costs $23,000 per year. A savings of almost 50%. And we know it works—PSH has a 93% success rate."

COVID-19 has compounded the challenges in the city's homeless services system. Shelters experienced outbreaks of the coronavirus, requiring emergency measures by providers and requiring the city to isolate and separate the most vulnerable of the homeless population. Staff proximity to clients resulted in many having to go into quarantine, which compounded staff shortages.

Homeward DC 2.0

Based on experience from Homeward DC 1.0, the District has advanced and plans to officially release Homeward DC 2.0 by early 2021, its strategic plan for the next five years through 2025. Homeward DC 2.0 is the result of a highly collaborative process led by the ICH in 2019 and early 2020 with some additional revisions made following the onset of the COVID-19 public health emergency. The federal government has defined an end to homelessness to mean that "every community will have a systematic response in place that ensures homelessness is prevented whenever possible, or is otherwise a rare, brief, and non-recurring experience." In accordance with this definition, the city has established its vision to end long-term homelessness and to create a system that quickly stabilizes households that do experience housing loss and connects them back to permanent housing as quickly as possible. The vision of the Homeward DC 2.0 strategic plan is that "Homelessness in the District of Columbia will be rare, brief, and nonrecurring, with focus on eliminating racial inequities and creating systemic fair treatment of all persons."

Some key points and principles of the plan as proposed are highlighted here:

- Structure and racial inequities are a root cause of homelessness. People of color are dramatically overrepresented among those experiencing homelessness. Historical and persistent racial discrimination in housing, employment, healthcare, education, criminal justice, and other systems contribute to high rates of homelessness for people of color.

- Trauma is both a cause and consequence of homelessness. The entire system must acknowledge this reality and be trained to provide trauma-informed services.
- DC will continue to embrace the Housing First philosophy as a system. Further, while this plan is focused more on the resources and policy changes required within the homeless services system, significant and sustained investment in affordable housing throughout the District, particularly for low-income households at or below 30 percent of Area Median Income (AMI), will be essential to increasing housing stability in D.C.
- Better coordination of mainstream anti-poverty programs is critical to create a stronger safety net and to prevent individuals and families from losing their housing in the first place, especially at transition points between youth and adult systems of care.
- There is strength in collaboration. The Plan highlights that government has a significant role in ending homelessness, but other partners must be at the table, too. It also identifies the important role of developers who are willing to provide affordable housing, landlords who are willing to rent to households that have experienced homelessness, and employers who are willing to hire them. The Plan also encourages faith-based partners and other community groups to consider how they can provide mentoring and moral support to struggling neighbors.

Under Homeward DC 2.0, the analysis assumes that just over one-quarter of new singles inflow will need PSH to resolve their homelessness. But because the majority of PSH resources allocated to the system in any given year is used to serve current chronically homeless individuals first, it is assumed in the plan analysis that virtually all individuals in this new inflow needing PSH will move to the long-term/chronic category in the subsequent year since sufficient PSH housing resources do not currently exist. This assumption is supported by recent system experience with hundreds of chronically homeless individuals exiting the streets or shelter to PSH each year but with the city's chronically homeless PIT number just barely declining.

Unfortunately, experience shows that the longer people are stuck in shelter and/or sleeping on the street, the more their situations deteriorate, and the more intervention is needed. The analysis for Homeward DC 2.0 shows that at current investment levels over the next five years, although hundreds of individuals would move from homelessness to permanent housing, the current chronic homelessness population would decrease by less than half, and new inflow requiring PSH would not be accommodated. Further, the analysis shows little reduction in the number of shelter beds needed for the individual homeless population. Clearly, increased investment will be needed to make substantial inroads in reducing singles' long-term homelessness. Unfortunately, COVID-19 has put severe constraints on the City's budget and only 214 PSH units for singles are included in the FY2021 budget, well below current needs.

Additionally, the past five years has shown that a growing number of seniors are experiencing first-time homelessness and that there is a higher level of vulnerability among the new inflow than previously thought. Also, given that the single-adult population is an aging one, the city has identified the need for housing options that offer more intensive, on-site support, suggesting that a significant portion of future investments in

PSH will need to be in group facilities where on-site support can more efficiently and effectively be provided.

The plan also highlights that approximately 60,000 households in the District are severely rent-burdened, and therefore any household crisis can often lead to housing loss. With Covid-19 impacts on jobs and income, there is a significantly increased threat of evictions and increased homelessness. This underscores the importance of homelessness prevention programming in addition to accommodating existing demand, and the District plans to continue placing emphasis on prevention. Separate from the plan, Mayor Bowser also recently set a goal for more housing production in DC to keep up with area job growth: 36,000 units by 2025, with a goal of one-third of the units being affordable.

N Street Village Example of Holistic Approach to Women's Homelessness

N Street Village in DC was founded by my church, Luther Place, in 1972. Originally a mission of the church, NSV is now a DC social service nonprofit with the mission to empower low-income and homeless women to claim their highest quality of life and to directly provide or assist women in getting affordable housing. NSV accomplishes its mission by offering a portfolio of services designed to meet the needs of its clients. These services are currently offered at eight physical locations in DC, with the flagship building located at Fourteenth and N Street NW across from Luther Place church.

In the years after the fiery devastation in the local community following the assassination of Dr. Martin Luther King in April 1968 (see accompanying photo), Luther Place began to consider its property and location as an opportunity to help minister to the wounded of the city. It began transforming dilapidated row houses in the church property on N Street into what would become a smorgasbord of faith-inspired service programs (Bread for the City; Deborah's Place, a house for women in transition; Zacchaeus Medical Clinic; Bethany Women's Day Center, etc.) to help bring healing in the community. A multi-denominational religious community led by Luther Place, with a Protestant, Jewish, and Catholic coalition (ProJeCt), gradually created what was to become known as N Street Village. A critical step along the way was Luther Place's opening of its church doors to the homeless in the cold winter of 1976. From that event in the winter of 1976, there was no turning back. The interfaith ministry to homeless women grew and eventually became a full continuum of services for women coming out of homelessness.

Northwest DC after MLK assassination in April 1968 (Photo by Warren K. Leffler, Library of Congress public collection)

Through dedicated and persistent leadership, in December 1996 the community celebrated the opening of a major new facility at Fourteenth and N Street NW that included Promise Place, housing the continuum of programs for homeless women, and Eden House, fifty-one apartments serving low- and moderate-income individuals and families (see accompanying picture).

N Street Village flagship building at Fourteenth and N Street NW, DC

This facility, along with the Luther Place Night Shelter, formed the core of N Street Village until recent years, when additional programs at other locations in the city became part of the Village. NSV acquired Miriam's House for women with HIV/AIDS in 2011 through a merger; the property has undergone major renovation and now provides PSH for twenty-five women in Northwest DC. In 2012 NSV contracted with the city to manage Erna's House in Northwest DC, which houses thirty-one chronically homeless women under the city's Housing First policy (which takes the most chronically homeless off the street and gives them housing first before dealing with their other challenges). In 2016, forty years after the opening of its first shelter in the basement of Luther Place and twenty years after opening its flagship property across Fourteenth Street from the church, NSV was selected to manage a major short-term emergency housing operation for women in downtown DC, at the renovated Patricia Handy Place for Women located in Chinatown at 810 Fifth Street NW. The shelter, which provides 213 beds for single women, replaced the old Federal City Shelter. My wife Margaret and I sometimes volunteer to serve meals at the Pat Handy facility, and it brings back memories of serving at the opening of NSV's first homeless shelter in the basement of our church in that cold winter of 1976, when so many homeless people were dying on the streets. NSV has come a long way in providing the full range of services needed to help so many women restore the wholeness of life, but unfortunately, there are still many people falling through the cracks in our nation's capital.

NSV has continued to expand and modify its services to homeless women in recent years as part of the citywide effort of Homeward DC to end chronic homelessness. The flagship building at Fourteenth and N Street NW provides permanent supportive housing with embedded services to forty-four women who are coping with mental health issues, addiction, trauma, physical health problems, or other issues that require support to help them remain stably housed. Residents live in studio or shared apartments and enjoy social and therapeutic activities provided by the Village. The flagship location also provides recovery housing in a therapeutic community program for up to twenty-one women with co-occurring mental illness and addiction. Women work to stabilize their mental health and recovery with the support of each other, their recovery networks, and NSV staff. The flagship location includes a wellness center that offers integrated mental health, physical health, and addiction recovery services to homeless and low-income women. The center takes a holistic approach to wellness, offering a full spectrum of daily wellness programs that promote health education, physical fitness, and holistic well-being. Three in five women arrive at NSV with no income. The NSV goal is to meet a client where she is and provide opportunities for income and employment growth through a variety of programs. NSV also recognizes the importance of community in the healing and recovery process and therefore promotes peer mentorship and peer leadership programs that help women feel connected and empowered. The NSV flagship location recently opened the MARJ & MAK Vocational Center. The vocational center provides drop-in classes as well as one-on-one trainings to support women in reaching their goals related to education, employment, benefits, income, and/or financial health.

NSV is also providing services for permanent housing for women since the 2018 renovation of the Phyllis Wheatley YWCA site at ninth and Rhode Island Avenue NW. This facility houses eighty women in single room occupancy (SRO) units with NSV selected to provide supportive services to about half of these women. Two additional properties have been recently added where NSV has partnered with developers to provide services for permanent low-income housing as well as a new women's shelter to deal with the COVID-19 impact, and a new Rapid Re-housing program for single women.

- **Capital Vista**- The Dantes Partners-led project provides for 2,730 square feet of retail space along with affordable units at 30 percent and 50 percent of area median income (AMI) located at 810 New Jersey Avenue NW. NSV will provide intensive case management services to 21 women that were chronically homeless. These women will occupy the 21 PSH units that include 11 efficiencies and 10 one bedrooms.

- **Diane's House**- This newly opened development in northeast DC provides 42 units for individuals, and single mother families at risk for homelessness. The District of Columbia Housing Authority is providing 39 project-based vouchers to low-income residents. Thirty-nine (39) of the 42 units are PSH and 33 units are one bedroom for women experiencing homelessness and six are two-bedroom units for single women experiencing homelessness and one child. NSV is providing intensive case management services for the women with children and the single adult women who will be residing in this new PSH program.
- **Adams Place**- Due to COVID-19, current shelters including Pat Handy had to significantly reduce the number of clients to allow safe accommodations. For homeless women this resulted in insufficient shelter capacity and the need to open another facility. NSV was requested by the city to operate an additional 30 bed shelter for women in Northeast Washington which opened in late 2020. This 30-bed facility provides onsite day programming and case management services as well. NSV is working with its government partners to implement the housing assistance process for women as they are matched to PSH or Rapid Re-Housing while at Adams Place.
- **Rapid Re-Housing** (RRH) for single homeless women- DC is ramping up its support for RRH for singles and NSV has received 2020 funding to implement such a program for the first time. Staffing and program development are underway. This program will serve 17

chronically homeless women in scattered site apartments operated by private landlords and property management. NSV has hired a housing specialist and is beginning the landlord engagement to help advocate for women that would be successful in RRH.

These expansions, in addition to NSV's acquisition of Miriam's House in 2011 and opening of Erna's House in 2012, are all very important steps toward expanding critical resources for homeless and low-income women in our city. But the challenge of getting more of the women into permanent housing is still daunting. DC is one of the most expensive rental markets in the country. This is so evident along the Fourteenth Street corridor, where my church created NSV over forty-five years ago to respond to the then massive rise in homelessness. The Fourteenth Street corridor in the early 1970s was a blighted area with marginal businesses, extensive drug trafficking and prostitution, and a growing homeless population. Now today, it is one of the hottest developing corridors in the District, with high-end housing, retail, restaurants, bars, and theaters and virtually twenty-four-hour activity. This increases the challenge for NSV and other providers to find affordable permanent housing for the homeless and formerly homeless.

Schroeder Stribling, CEO of N Street Village, and co-chair of the D.C. Interagency Council on Homelessness Executive Committee says, "Every day at least one woman comes to N Street Village for the first time, and I know that – but for a few circumstances of fortune and timing – 'she' could be me."

Evelyn Green, former director of Bethany Day Center and now director of Greenhouse at N Street Village

Evelyn came to N Street Village as a homeless woman nearly thirty years ago, after many years on the street. She was able to repair her own life at the Village but also wanted to give back to other women who came through the doors. She became a staff person twenty-five years ago and is still at NSV, mentoring other women coming out of homelessness in recently appointed position as director of Greenhouse, which is named after her.

The interfaith example of NSV's founding and long years of service to homeless women, the diligent work of the interfaith advocacy group Washington Interfaith Network (WIN) to successfully advocate for more affordable housing, and a particular WIN campaign a few years ago to pressure the city to replace the crowded family shelter at DC General show the power of faith in action. Communities of faith have been at the forefront of justice initiatives for "the least of these" in DC for more than half a century since the tragic events surrounding the assassination of Dr. Martin Luther King Jr. in 1968. Now, with the devasting impacts of COVID-19, the challenge for advocates and providers has been further magnified as many homeless and low-income families and individuals face increased health and economic risk.

6

Human/Civil Rights

Human rights are generally thought of as basic rights and freedoms that all people are entitled to regardless of nationality, sex, age, national or ethnic origin, race, religion, language, or other status, as embedded in international law in the 1948 United Nations Universal Declaration of Human Rights. The UN Declaration includes the right to life and liberty, freedom from slavery and torture, freedom of opinion and expression, the right to work and education, and more. Civil rights, on the other hand, are those rights that one enjoys by virtue of citizenship in a particular nation or state, and they generally protect citizens from discrimination. President Franklin Roosevelt once said about these rights, "We must scrupulously guard the civil rights and civil liberties of all our citizens, whatever their background. We must remember that any oppression, any injustice, any hatred, is a wedge designed to attack our civilization."

Although the Declaration of Independence stated that we all are created equal and have certain inalienable rights, it has been a long struggle for many groups within our society to fully realize these rights. Women's suffrage was a long struggle, with support from the Social Gospel movement helping to achieve women's voting rights in 1920. In 1972, the Equal Rights Amendment (ERA) to the Constitution was passed by Congress but failed to get ratification from two-thirds of the states (note: Virginia's recent approval of the ERA revives hope for the amendment, but legal questions remain), but women nevertheless have made impressive gains in regard to equal protection in the workplace and other fronts. Regarding race, it has been an exceedingly long struggle. Our founding Constitution embedded slavery without ever mentioning the word. The Constitution's three-fifths clause counted those enslaved as only three-fifths of a person. The Constitution forbid any attempt to ban the nation's international slave trade for twenty years after its enactment in 1787. Although the international slave trade was ended by Federal legislation in 1807, the domestic slave trade continued unabated for decades after. Despite the Emancipation Proclamation by Lincoln and the equal protection provisions of the Fourteenth Amendment in 1868, nearly a hundred years later, in 1949, theologian Howard Thurman laid bare the continuing racial inequality in the United States in his book *Jesus and the Disinherited*. His book became an inspiration for Dr. Martin Luther King Jr. and the civil rights movement, which helped lead to the Civil Rights Act of 1964 and the Voting Rights Act of 1965, among other accomplishments. Despite impressive gains, issues of gender, race, human sexuality, and immigrant assimilation still tear at the fabric of American society.

Isabel Wilkerson's recent book, *Caste: The Origins of Our Discontents*, is a thorough and wrenching documentation of America's racist history. She intertwines caste and race and finds that caste is a more applicable term for our repressive history. A caste system, she writes, is "an artificial construction, a fixed and embedded ranking of human value that sets the presumed supremacy of one group against the presumed inferiority of other groups on the basis of ancestry and often immutable traits, traits that would be neutral in the abstract but are ascribed life-and-death meaning." An insightful point she makes about the white working class twice voting strongly for Trump is that, even though some of his policies like healthcare were often against their social or economic interests, they still voted for him to preserve the caste system and their pecking order in that system. She discusses the cruel logic of caste which requires that there be a bottom rung(s) against which those in the lower middle rungs of the economic and social ladder can measure themselves.

One of our nation's challenges is the uneasiness that segments of our population feel about the emerging diversity of our country. Kenneth Prewitt, former director of the US Census Bureau, has said of the US that "we're on our way to becoming the first country in history that is literally made up of every part of the world." Asian American and mixed-race people have recently become the two fastest-growing segments of the US population, while the number of non-Hispanic whites is decreasing. According to census data, the big shift in demographics reached a milestone in 2011, when, for the first time, more racial-minority babies than white babies were born in the US. From now on, we will have an increasingly Black, brown, Asian, and immigrant population, and it is projected that by 2055, the US will not have a single racial or ethnic majority. Millennials have just surpassed baby boomers as the largest US adult generation, and they differ significantly from their elders in many ways. They are the most racially diverse adult generation in American history, with 43 percent of millennials being nonwhite.

Embrace of this increasing diversity is a challenge, and we have seen recent backlash, particularly against immigrants. It is encouraging that recent Pew Research Center surveys have found that more a majority of Americans say immigrants strengthen the country and that increasing ethnic diversity makes it a better place to live. But there is definitely a partisan divide. A Public Religion Research Institute survey released in July 2018 found that although 64 percent of Americans regard increasing demographic diversity as mostly positive, Democrats believe that it is mostly positive by an overwhelming margin of 85 to 13 percent, as do independents by 59 to 34 percent, but 50 percent of Republicans regard it as mostly negative, compared to only 43 percent who favor it. In recent decades, minority groups and women have increasingly advocated for their rights while working-class whites, particularly males, have expressed feelings of being left behind, and this in part contributed to a surprising outcome in the 2016 presidential election. The PRRI survey results suggest that the key drivers of these partisan divisions are educational and religious, and I would add geography to these, given that metropolitan areas are much more diverse than rural areas. Sixty-nine percent of whites with a college degree have a mostly positive view of demographic diversity, compared to just 50 percent of whites without college degrees.

The challenge looking forward is how to create a broad national identity centered on core American ideas and values rather than narrow ethnic, racial, or religious ones. We need to focus on and celebrate more of the things that make us all proud of being American. Demographer William H. Frey is convinced that if we can just get our acts together when it comes to race, America will thrive. Frey, best known for his 2014 book *Diversity Explosion: How New Racial Demographics Are Remaking America*, writes, "I am convinced that the United States is in the midst of a pivotal period ushering in extraordinary shifts in the nation's racial demographic makeup. If planned for properly, these demographic changes will allow the country to face the future with growth and vitality as it reinvents the classic

American melting pot for a new era." The evidence is mounting that geographical openness and cultural diversity and tolerance are key drivers of economic progress.

Racial Discrimination

On top of the COVID-19 pandemic, our country has been confronted with what many describe as a second pandemic, that of systemic racism. Racism has been present since our country's founding but in 2020 the issue was visually brought to our consciousness in a way that cannot be denied. The gruesome video of George Floyd's death in May 2020 as a Minneapolis police officer knelt on his neck for some nine minutes precipitated a national reckoning around racism. Floyd's killing, coming on top of other recent nationally visible wrongful killings of Blacks, resulted in demonstrations in scores of cities across the country led by the Black Lives Matter (BLM) movement. Some see similarities to demonstrations that erupted a half century ago after the assassination of the Rev. Martin Luther King Jr. That tragic historic moment led to President Lyndon Johnson challenging racial housing discrimination and Congress passing the Housing and Urban Development Act of 1968. Housing reform came on top of the Civil Rights and Voting Rights legislation in 1964-65.

When late-night host Stephen Colbert asked African American author Ta-Nehisi Coates on *The Late Show*, "Do you have any hope … about how we could be a better country, we could have better race relations, we could have better politics?" Coates could not offer any hope. Coates, who writes on race issues for the *Atlantic*, does not seem to believe that America is going to "get over" racism. In his pessimistic outlook, he says that "white supremacy is so foundational to America that it will be impossible to ever eradicate it." White supremacy is undeniably a part of the history of America, its founders, and its founding documents. Slavery was inextricably linked to this white dominance, and we fought a civil war largely over the issue of slavery.

From the time Europeans arrived on American shores, they exploited the land and its inhabitants. The US government itself authorized an untold number of wars, attacks, and raids on Native Americans. By the close of the Frontier Wars in the late nineteenth century, fewer than 238,000 indigenous people remained, a sharp decline from the estimated 5 million to 15 million living in North America when Columbus arrived in 1492. Belief in white superiority over the supposedly inferior natives allowed this massive slaughter of the Native Americans. From 1830 to 1840, the US Army removed approximately 60,000 Native American from the East in "exchange" for new territory west of the Mississippi. Thousands died along the way in what became known as the Trail of Tears; it was authorized by US President Andrew Jackson with the complicity of all our governmental institutions and citizenry.

We would do well to reflect on what Frederick Douglass said in his famous 1852 Rochester, New York, Independence Day speech on the occasion of the nation's seventy-sixth birthday: "This Fourth July is yours, not mine. You may rejoice, I must mourn ... What, to the American slave, is your Fourth of July? I answer, a day that reveals to him, more than all other days in the year, the gross injustice and cruelty to which he is the constant victim." Douglass ended his 1852 Fourth of July speech on an optimistic note, saying, "Knowledge is too readily available, and soon the American people will open their eyes to the atrocities they have been inflicting on their fellow Americans." Douglass that day could not foresee that we would soon fight a brutal civil war over the issue of slavery, and although Lincoln emancipated enslaved people, the long history of racism would persist in America. Here we are almost two centuries later having witnessed a President who began his ascendancy to power by invoking the racist birther campaign against our first African American president, Barak Obama. And Trump's "Make America Great Again" campaign slogan clearly harkened back to a time of white patriarchal dominance. We must be honest about our history and recognize that the racial division and white nationalism we see today have always been a part of our nation's history and will not be so easily erased.

We must note also that white supremacy is a part of the history of American Christianity, as are abolition and support for civil rights. Clashes over race have roiled congregations for as long as they have been in America. Some white Christians, particularly Quakers, were often at the forefront of antislavery movements in nineteenth-century America, but most white Christians were not. White churches in the South vigorously defended the practice of slavery. In 1864, for example, the General Assembly of the Presbyterian Church in the Confederate States of America declared that "the long-continued agitations of our adversaries have wrought within us a deeper conviction of the divine appointment of domestic servitude. We hesitate not to affirm that it is the peculiar mission of the Southern Church to conserve the institution of slavery, and to make it a blessing both to master and slave."

The Union victory in the Civil War, Emancipation, and postwar Reconstruction provided a temporary reprieve in white dominance of Blacks in the South. We saw the passage of remarkable civil rights amendments to the Constitution between 1865 and 1870:

- the Thirteenth Amendment, abolishing all forms of slavery.
- the Fourteenth Amendment, granting citizenship and the promise of equal protection under the law; and
- the Fifteenth Amendment, granting the right to vote for Black men.

The Reconstruction period saw former enslaved people using their newly earned constitutional rights as Americans to serve in interracial governments that came to power in the former Confederacy as well as to win election to national offices. But the sight of formerly enslaved people eagerly lining up to vote and electing their fellow citizens to public offices was appalling to many Southerners, who had relied on and justified slavery and believed that "Negroes" were inferior and unfit for office. The Klan and other white supremacy resistance groups emerged by the late 1860s. Southern resistance and northern indifference led to the gradual abandonment of Reconstruction. This stands as one of the great tragedies of American history. Lynching became a major tool of white supremacists to intimidate Black people after Reconstruction. According to the Tuskegee Institute, 4,743 people were lynched between 1882 and 1968, predominately African American men. It would be another hundred years after Reconstruction before the civil rights era of the 1960s would bring enactment of major new civil rights legislation including the 1964 Civil Rights Act, the 1965 Voting Rights Act, and the Fair Housing Act of 1968. Housing discrimination became a government sponsored enterprise particularly with the suburban housing boom after World War II. The Federal Housing Administration (FHA) guidelines said that "incompatible racial groups should not be permitted to live in the same communities", a not-so-subtle implication that African Americans or other minorities were not welcome in the emerging suburbs. At the same time, a practice known as 'redlining' emerged where Black neighborhoods were literally colored red on city maps to denote areas that were considered too risky to be insured by federal loans. Loans in these neighborhoods were unavailable or very expensive, making it more difficult for low-income minorities to buy homes and setting the stage for the country's persistent racial wealth gap that still exists. White families were able to use their appreciating suburban home equities to send their children to college and were able to bequeath wealth to their children. None of those advantages accrued to African Americans who were largely trapped in redlined inner-city neighborhoods.

It was a more than a half century ago, in February 1968, after much racial unrest, that the Kerner Commission report on racial unrest was released. The commission's report concluded that racial unrest was a product of a wide range of injustices, ranging from inadequate schools and housing to poverty-wage jobs and discriminatory treatment from police and the criminal justice system. In the words of the report, "White racism is essentially responsible for the explosive mixture which has been accumulating in our cities since the end of World War II." The report's prescription to prevent further unrest included large-scale investments in housing, education, and employment. Rather than heed the commission's call for investments to remedy the conditions that had led to unrest, the country's power structure instead tried to control and punish the victims of those conditions with a law-and-order approach. The US embarked on an unprecedented and dramatic expansion of its prison system with disproportionate mass incarceration of African Americans.

In the 1970s and 1980s, an increase in crime along with the

tragic "war on drugs" led to a bipartisan push to greatly expand prison sentences. And mandatory minimum drug sentences enacted in the mid-1980s caused a dramatic increase in the number of offenders going to prison and the length of time spent behind bars. This was not primarily a problem of overzealous police and prosecutors; rather, we as a society largely supported and condoned it. With over 2 million people now imprisoned, the United States, with 5 percent of the world's total population, holds 25 percent of the world's prison population. In his October 2015 Atlantic magazine article "The Black Family in the Age of Mass Incarceration," Ta-Nehisi Coates says, "From the mid-70s to the mid-80s, America's incarceration rate doubled. From the mid-80s to the mid-90s it doubled again. Then it went still higher." Coates highlights the devastating impact of mass incarceration on Black families. He says one in four Black men born since the late 70s has spent time in prison. Author Michelle Alexander says in her book *The New Jim Crow: Mass Incarceration in the Age of Colorblindness* that "the only country that comes close to America's rate of incarceration is Russia, and no other country in the world incarcerates such an astonishing number of its racial and ethnic minorities." These authors suggest that mass incarceration pushed thousands of Black men out of the job market, disqualified them from food stamps, increased their risk of homelessness, and increased their risk of being incarcerated again. And with this high rate of imprisonment of Black men, already vulnerable Black families and the women who sustain them were plummeted into greater poverty, stress, and strain when their loved ones were incarcerated.

Another perverse aspect of incarceration is that a huge private, for-profit prison industry has emerged. Mother Jones magazine reports that today, the $5 billion industry houses close to 20 percent of federal prisoners, and private prisons are increasingly being used as immigration detention centers. The industry lobbies politicians because of the financial stake they have; meanwhile, these private companies have seen their revenue and market share soar. This business model depends on high rates of incarceration. Nearly two-thirds of private prison contracts mandate that state and local governments maintain a certain occupancy rate—often 90 percent or more—or require taxpayers to pay for empty beds. Further, under this private prison system, inmates are often exploited to provide cheap labor for some of the most profitable companies in the world.

There is some recent good news regarding incarceration: rates have dropped somewhat in the last decade, and the racial disparity has diminished, mostly because of action at the state level. Some thirty states have enacted policies to reverse corrections growth and contain costs. The April 2019 annual report from the Bureau of Justice Statistics shows that the number of prisoners under state or federal jurisdiction in 2017 had dropped to 1.48 million people, down from 1.61 million in 2009. With increased national attention regarding mass incarceration, Congress finally initiated some reforms. Having attempted more comprehensive reform in the past and failed, Congress pursued more modest legislation. The bill, called the First Step Act, passed in December 2018 with wide bipartisan support, applies only to the federal system. It very slightly pulls back punitive mandatory minimum sentences and provides new funding for education and rehabilitation programs, but much more remains to be done.

Here in the twenty-first century, after the nation twice elected an African American president, the issue of race is increasingly in the headlines in recent years. In 2016, we elected a president who led the "birther" movement questioning then President Obama's native birth and whose "Make America Great Again" campaign helped inspire a resurgence of white nationalism. We now seem to be in a period of backlash (many note parallels to the post-Reconstruction period), with the increase of white nationalist groups, voting restrictions and gerrymandering that often disadvantage African Americans and other minorities, and increased racially motivated violence. As noted previously, the mid-2017 Charlottesville protests over dismantling Confederate monuments were a stark demonstration of the backlash, as white nationalists including neo-Nazis rallied with hate speech and violence, including the death of a young woman at the hands of a white nationalist. President Trump, in a subsequent press conference question about Charlottesville, responded that there "were very fine people, on both sides"!

In response to nationally publicized police and vigilante-type killings and increased racial hate incidents, the Black Lives Matter (BLM) movement has emerged in recent years with a mission to build local power and to intervene in violence inflicted on Black communities. BLM has become an international activist movement and regularly speaks out on issues such as racial profiling, police brutality, and racial inequality in the US criminal justice system. The phrase "All Lives Matter" also

> The pleading voice of George Floyd as he was gasping for breath under the knee of a white police officer: **"I can't breathe!"**

sprang up as a pushback against BLM. Of course, all lives matter, but such slogans diminish our brutal racial history. It has been said that "All Lives Matter only when Black Lives Matter". It is becoming clearer to America that racism was not solved by Lincoln's Emancipation Proclamation, the Civil Rights Era, or the election of its first Black President in 2008. It is a problem still with us as has been painfully revealed in the recent police and vigilante killings of unarmed Blacks and the massive protests that have arisen across the nation and beyond in the summer of 2020. It is a sad commentary that it took a cellphone video of a Black man, George Floyd, cruelling dying at the hands of a white policeman to make a majority of white Americans decide that this might be enough.

Bryan Stevenson's book and movie documentary, *Just Mercy*, are highly recommended to all concerned about racial justice. His painful stories of false incarceration and executions of African Americans require us to admit that our approach to criminal law is cruel and inhumane. Stevenson is the executive director of the Equal Justice Initiative (EJI) in Montgomery, Alabama. He has won relief for dozens of condemned prisoners, including several on death row; has argued five times before the Supreme Court, notably on behalf of juvenile prisoners; and has won national acclaim for his work challenging bias in our criminal justice system against the poor and people of color. EJI is committed to ending mass incarceration and excessive punishment in the United States, to challenging racial and economic injustice, and to protecting basic human rights for the most vulnerable people in American society.

Desmond Tutu, Nobel Peace Prize laureate, says,

> Bryan Stevenson is America's young Nelson Mandela, a brilliant lawyer fighting with courage and conviction to guarantee justice for all. *Just Mercy* should be read by people of conscience in every civilized country in the world to discover what happens when revenge and retribution replace justice and mercy. It is as gripping to read as any legal thriller, and what hangs in the balance is nothing less than the soul of a great nation.

The key message of Stevenson's book is that with determined struggle, evil can be overcome. *Just Mercy* will upset you, but it will also make you hopeful. Stevenson makes an important point about "proximity." He says that "proximity to anything will give you nuances and insight that you can't get at a distance. My proximity to these men and women on death row show me parts of their humanity and parts of their character, their redemptive potential." For me personally, being proximate to homeless women for over forty-five years at Luther Place and N Street Village has given me insights about poverty, abuse, mental illness, addiction, and the like that I never would have had otherwise and has made me an activist for social justice. Bryan Stevenson concludes with this challenge to us all, "We will ultimately not be judged by our technology, we won't be judged by our design, we won't be judged by our intellect and reason. Ultimately, you judge the character of a society … by how they treat the poor, the condemned, the incarcerated."

In recent years, Stevenson took on a project that he hopes can lead to deeper examination of our racial history and help lead toward healing. The EJI planned and built a national memorial, the Peace and Justice Memorial in Montgomery, Alabama, which recounts the history of slavery and lynching in America. Our family recently took a remarkable journey to visit the memorial and its companion Legacy Museum, both opened in April 2018. EJI believes that the history of racial inequality and economic injustice in the United States has not been fully acknowledged and that racial reconciliation cannot happen until we are honest about our past. The Legacy Museum: From Enslavement to Mass Incarceration is built on the site of a former warehouse where enslaved Black people were imprisoned and is located midway between a historic slave market and the main river dock and train station where tens of thousands of enslaved people were trafficked during the height of the domestic slave trade. The National Memorial for Peace and Justice forces a reckoning with one of the nation's least recognized atrocities: the lynching of thousands of Black people in a decades-long campaign of racist terror. Lynching was a tool used to oppress Black people after the Civil War (see the accompanying photo of the memorial sculpture). The lynchings were often committed by mobs who murdered victims with impunity, often in the presence of law enforcement or on courthouse lawns.

The National Memorial for Peace and Justice (Kwame Akoto-Bamfo, Nkyinkyim Installation, 2018; Montgomery, Alabama)

EJI collected soil from the more than four thousand lynching sites throughout the South and beyond, and the jars of soil are part of an exhibit that tells the stories of lynching victims. Stevenson speaks about the power of soil. "In this soil, there is the sweat of the enslaved. In the soil there is the blood of victims of racial violence and lynching. There are tears in the soil from all those who labored under the indignation and humiliation of segregation. But in the soil, there is also the opportunity for new life, a chance to grow something hopeful and healing for the future." EJI believes it is essential that we begin to discuss our history of racial injustice more soberly and to understand the implications of our past in addressing the challenges of the present. James Cone, author of *The Cross and the Lynching Tree*, says that until whites, and particularly white Christians, come to grips with the history of lynching and the church's complicity, there can be no reconciliation.

Since the 2014 publication of Ta-Nehisi Coates's *Atlantic* article "The Case for Reparations," arguing that reparations would drive a "national reckoning that would lead to spiritual renewal," there has been increased discussion of the issue. Coates articulated in his article the great wealth gap between Black and white families. He cited the Pew Research Center estimates that white households are worth roughly twenty times as much as Black households and that more than a third of Black households do not have a safety net at all for times of emergency. Conservative columnist David Brooks discussed reparations in a 2019 opinion piece. He said that while there have been many types of discrimination in our history, the African America experience is unique. Brooks reflected that slavery, and the long continuing pattern of racial discrimination is at the core of the racial economic disparities and divisiveness we see today. Finally, he stated that although reparations are a drastic policy and hard to implement, "the very act of talking about and designing them heals a wound and opens a new story."

In September 2014, a Georgetown University junior published a column in the *Hoya*, the student newspaper, with the headline "Georgetown, Financed by Slave Trading." It unearthed a largely forgotten history: that the esteemed Jesuit university had saved itself from financial ruin in 1838 by selling 272 enslaved people. This started a five-year debate over how the school should atone for its slaveholding past. In 2016, the university agreed to give admissions preference to descendants of the 272 enslaved, and the first two descendants arrived in the fall of 2017. College officials and the Jesuits held a mass of contrition in the spring of 2017 as a formal apology for the university's actions regarding enslaved peoples. But the issue has not gone away, and in April 2019 Georgetown University students voted overwhelmingly for a proposal to create a fund to help descendants of the enslaved people the school sold in the nineteenth century. In September 2019, Virginia Theological Seminary announced it had set up a $1.7 million fund to provide reparations. The Alexandria, Virginia, Episcopal seminary acknowledged that it once had used enslaved labor and supported segregation, citing this history as part of the reason it wanted to provide restitution.

On April 3–5, 2018, the National Council of the Churches of Christ (NCC) in the US and other interfaith partners gathered in Washington, DC, for a historic event to launch their Truth and Racial Justice Initiative. As the nation marked fifty years since the assassination of Rev. Dr. Martin Luther King Jr. on April 4, 1968, the faith community committed to help eradicate the entrenched racism that still grips the US and limits our ability to see every human being as equal. Representatives from eighteen religious traditions attended the events. The presiding bishop of the Evangelical Lutheran Church of America (ELCA), Elizabeth Eaton, attended and while in DC paid a visit to my church, Luther Place. She is pictured in the accompanying image on the left, along with my pastor Reverend Karen Brau on the right and yours truly in the middle. The NCC and partners challenged themselves and others to join in truth-telling, leading to actions that right the wrongs and bring healing and wholeness to all people and unity to the nation.

ELCA supporting the Truth and Racial Justice Initiative of the National Council of Churches

My own Lutheran national church body, the ELCA, issued an official apology in June 2019 to people of African descent for its history of complicity in slavery and its legacy of racism, on the four hundredth anniversary of the first forced transatlantic voyage of enslaved African people. The church statement lamented that the white Lutheran church in America had not worked actively for the abolition of slavery, had perpetuated racism in the church, and too often had been silent in the face of racial injustice. This was in response to a 2015 call by the African Descent Lutheran Association to the ELCA for a statement of repentance regarding this long history of complicity in racism by the white Lutheran church.

Now in 2020 and into early 2021, we sadly have witnessed the disproportionate impact of the coronavirus pandemic on minorities followed by multiple high-profile police killings of African Americans which resulted in continuing nationwide protests led by Black Lives Matter (BLM). Major pressure is building on police reform, addressing systemic racism. and transforming racial inequities in corporate America. The 'Defund Police' mission of BLM is controversial but there is clearly a great deal of support for police reform. It is critical to differentiate between the police and the services they provide. Regardless of what happens to police departments, states and cities must continue to fund most of the services that police departments have traditionally provided. Police are not trained and were not intended to do many of the jobs they are called on to perform. Police currently deal with such wide-ranging calls like mental illness, homelessness, domestic disputes, loud noise, and various non-criminal activities, on top of actual serious crime. Many functions performed by the police would be better done by others experienced with nonviolent community intervention. For example, homelessness, addiction, mental health, and domestic violence intervention is better accomplished by professionals in those fields rather than police. As an example of a new approach, Mayor Bowser in DC recently appointed a new deputy mayor for public safety and justice to oversee broad functions of public health, violence prevention, and policing among other related duties. Many believe the first order of business with police reform is to curb the militarization of police and the accompanying excessive use of force. Many cities are undertaking or considering reform and the Democratic led House of Representative passed a major bill in June 2020 titled the George Floyd Justice in Policing Act but has not been taken up in the Senate.

President Trump pushed back against BLM demonstrations, removal of confederate statues, and proposals to changes the names of military bases named after confederate generals. He pursued a divisive white nationalist agenda as part of his 2020 campaign rather than trying to bring the country together during a pandemic and great racial divide. Trump announced during the 2020 campaign that he was signing an executive order establishing the "1776 Commission" to promote a "patriotic education." Appealing to his white nationalist supporters, Trump said that the left is "attempting to destroy [the] beautiful vision" that the founding fathers had for America, and that things like the 1619 Project, which teach children about systemic racism and reframe the country's history by examining the consequences of slavery, are 'toxic propaganda' and 'ideological poison' that "if not removed, "will destroy our country." He went on to say, "Teaching this horrible doctrine to our children is a form of child abuse in the truest sense of those words" … "Patriotic moms and dads are going to demand that their children are no longer fed hateful lies about this country." The Commission notably included no historians and fortunately was immediately disbanded by President Biden on Inauguration Day.

In the days after George Floyd was killed, former President Barack Obama wrote, "For millions of Americans, being treated differently on account of race is tragically, painfully, maddeningly 'normal'." White America must finally accept that what has been normal for Blacks all these years has never been normal for whites. After centuries of white dominance, this hopefully is the tipping point for our country. "We have to get it right this time, or we risk losing our democracy forever" says author Michelle Alexander.

Women's Rights

From Thomas Jefferson's relationship with Sally Hemings to Bill Clinton's and Donald Trump's reputations for sexual improprieties, the list of executive officeholders and other prominent leaders who have been accused of sexual assault or misconduct is notable. Looking back to Thomas Jefferson's "relationship" with Sally Hemings, historians often have referred to her as his "mistress." In fact, Hemings was enslaved and history now reveals that Jefferson impregnated her with multiple children placed into slavery. The list of potential extramarital affairs by John F. Kennedy reportedly included one with Marilyn Monroe. Clinton's affair with Monica Lewinsky was the subject of dramatic impeachment proceedings. The most voluminous accusations against a president are those against former President Trump, who has been accused by more than twenty women of sexual harassment. Trump has denied these accusations, but the lewd *Access Hollywood* tape is virtually a self-admission of harassment.

In the past few years, we have seen numerous revelations of sexual harassment in politics, boardrooms, and newsrooms, with accusations and prominent media firings; the floodgates opened, and we seem to have reached a tipping point. After revelations about Hollywood movie producer Harvey Weinstein (who has now been convicted), more allegations surfaced in Hollywood, in sports, in business, in politics, and at media organizations, including National Public Radio. Charlie Rose, a prominent news commentator on PBS and CBS, was accused of blatant sexual-harassment conduct, leading to his release by both networks. This case was particularly shocking to me because I watched his show most every night and greatly admired his interviewing skills, but his revealed behavior was clearly reprehensive and deserving of punishment. We also saw accusations emerge regarding sitting politicians, including Senators Franken and Conyers and several congressmen, who were forced to resign. There was also the high-profile case of Jeffrey Epstein, who over the course of many years was accused of having sexually exploited and abused dozens of minor girls at his homes in Manhattan and Palm Beach, among other locations; he committed suicide while jailed.

Regarding where we go from here, I think that any current or prospective officeholder against whom there are substantial allegations of sexual harassment must immediately be investigated by the responsible government oversight bodies. In the case of Congress, which has one of the worst reputations among institutions for sexual harassment and abuse, there is a process for ethics investigation and dismissal for serious offenses, although it has been relatively ineffective. Current or future cases should promptly be taken up by the congressional ethics committees. Boardrooms and newsrooms are taking much swifter action regarding sexual harassment under mounting public pressure.

Attempts to control the reproductive lives of women too often stem from the structures of male dominance that we find in many of the major world religions. This is particularly problematic for women because when governments try politically to block women's access to reproductive health services, the government officials are often men raised in patriarchal religious traditions. In the United States these patriarchal views are most associated with the evangelical movement, which is the biggest voting bloc for Trump (who ironically characterized himself as "very pro-choice" before he considered running for office). The Roman Catholic Church also suffers from a strict patriarchal structure. The official position of the Catholic church on reproductive health matters, as restated in Pope John Paul II's 1995 encyclical "Evangelism Vitae," is that contraception, sterilization, abortion, and fertility treatments are attacks against life and are morally unacceptable. Catholic women do not abide by many of these strictures—for example, polls in the US show that Catholic women use contraception at or near the same rate as other women.

In 2019 we witnessed this patriarchal system when Alabama's totally male-dominated senate voted for a near total ban on women's reproductive rights, the strictest such law in the country. Georgia, Kentucky, Missouri, Mississippi, Ohio, and Louisiana also recently passed strict anti-abortion laws, so-called heartbeat bills, that effectively prohibit abortions after six to eight weeks of pregnancy. Unfortunately, these states do not seem to care nearly so much about children outside the womb. They often pursue family-destructive policies such as declining Medicaid expansion, cutting food and nutrition programs, and other such anti-poverty programs which are vitally needed among poor and working-class families. There is, of course, a long history in our country of male control over women's bodies. White male slaveowners had absolute right over the bodies of Black women, who were routinely raped and forbidden to prevent pregnancy. Any child born to an enslaved woman was a valued asset and was the sole property of the "master." Women's bodies then were—and still too often today are—viewed as a resource that men should be able to access freely without women having the right to refuse or the right to abort the baby a man put inside her. And sadly, these laws are being voted into effect by men who have trouble articulating the most basic facts about women's biology. When Alabama State Senator Clyde Chambliss was asked if the law would allow for incest victims to obtain abortions, he reportedly responded, "Yes, until she knows she's pregnant." What? And who can forget former Missouri congressman Todd Akin, who once claimed that women cannot get pregnant if they have been raped because "the female body has ways to shut the whole thing down." Women's bodies are quite literally in the hands of men who seemingly could not pass a high school health class.

The important hashtag #MeToo was born out of all these painful revelations and is helping thousands of women come forward who might have been too intimidated in the past to go public alone. The day after Trump's inauguration in January 2017, the Women's March became one of the largest demonstrations in American history; the march drew together hundreds of thousands of women from across the country, along with the men who supported them, to protest gender oppression and highlighted important gender issues such as affordable childcare, pay equity, job discrimination, sexual harassment, and reproductive rights. Many of these women returned home from the march and got involved in organizing for the first time in their lives. Issues that have been long ignored are finally coming to the surface, and women are increasingly speaking up and using their voices and influence to demand real change. When the *New York Times* exposed Harvey Weinstein's predations, it felt cathartic for women across the country. With the emergence of the #MeToo movement, it has become clear that women are not going to stay silent anymore.

Tracy Thomas, law professor at the University of Akron, points to the important role men have played in previous women's rights struggles. She cites the fight for women's suffrage, when male supporters added their voices in large numbers to finally get victory in 1920. She sees that support happening now and thinks it will be an important factor in changing the dynamics on the issue of sexual harassment. For meaningful change to happen, various education initiatives, including comprehensive training for staff and leadership of major public and private institutions about sexual harassment issues, are needed. The predominant practice on the Hill and in the corporate world of paying off victims and silencing them must end. Schools and campuses are an important place for multiple educational initiatives. It is time for society-wide reflection on how we can all contribute to making our social spaces and workspaces safe against harassment.

Despite great strides made by the international women's rights movement over many years, women and girls around the world are still forced into marriage as children or trafficked into forced labor and sex slavery. They are refused access to education and political participation, and some are trapped in conflicts where rape is perpetrated as a weapon of war. Around the world, deaths related to pregnancy and childbirth are needlessly high, and women are prevented from making deeply personal choices in their private lives.

Women's rights were among the key issues in the 2020 elections, and there were many women candidates and elected officials ready and willing to speak to these issues, building on success in the 2018 elections. The male old guard has been shaken up by new female lawmakers who are advancing bills particularly focused on women's health and safety.

Women have become more energized politically, not just because of pushback against sexual harassment, but because so many issues of importance to women and families are not being addressed. Emily's List, an organization devoted to electing female candidates, helped spur a record number of women to run for office in the 2018 midterm elections, and the Democrats sent the largest contingent of women ever to the House, over one hundred. Women thus made up nearly 40 percent of House Democrats in 2019, but less than 10 percent of House Republicans. Representation of women increased again in 2020 bringing hope for more civil debate and reduced tolerance for misogynist behavior among political leaders in Washington.

A further trend among the female electorate is that women of color are playing an increasing role in national politics. A recent report called *Ahead of the Majority*, based on Census data and voting patterns, found that since 2008, women of color have grown by eighteen percentage points in the general population and by twenty-five percentage points among registered voters.[52] Women of color voter turnout increased substantially in both the 2018 and 2020 elections and they heavily supported Democratic candidates.

White nationalists particularly fear the rise of women who are viewed as usurping traditional ale patriarch roles, and our president feeds on this same male anxiety about women of power. As revealed in an April 2018 analysis published by Diana C. Mutz of the University of Pennsylvania in the *Proceedings of the National Academy of Sciences*, Trump's election in part was a reflection of the dread that some white men seem to feel about their place in the world. In the wake of eight years under America's first Black president and faced with the prospect of the first female president, white men voted overwhelmingly for Trump, someone who openly displayed his misogyny. You can see this same fear reflected in white supremacists' attitudes toward minority advancements—if a Black person is doing well, it must mean a white person is losing. And rising outspoken women of color (like the so-called congressional "Squad") are seen as a particular threat because they highlight both feminist and racial minority advancement, seemingly to the disadvantage of white males. Trump clearly played on this fear to stir up his base.

Although women have made significant strides in the workforce in recent decades, when the economy crumbled with the pandemic, women were hit hardest. Women are still the primary low-income workers, the ones whose jobs tended to disappear when the coronavirus spread. Further, mothers have reduced their work hours disproportionately to fathers to care for their children during the pandemic. And Black women have been hit hardest; long-held, systemic racism coupled with the pandemic economic impacts has been most devastating for them. The devastating impacts of the lack of sick and broader family leave benefits in our country have been laid bare with COVID-19.

One hundred years after getting the right to vote, it is becoming increasingly clear that women are powering the vote in recent elections. Democrats won back control of the US House of Representatives in 2018, propelled in large part by women voters, and they were a key factor in giving Democrats the presidency in 2020. To help ensure turnout among women, groups such as Supermajority, led by Cecile Richards former head of Planned Parenthood and others formed coalitions over the last few years to further build women's power for advocacy, community building, and electoral participation, with the aim of transforming our country and building an intergenerational, multiracial movement for women's equity. Richards says, "Women's equality is at the forefront of people's minds in a way that it hasn't been ever in my history of looking at research and polling."

Gary E. Maring

Voting Rights

Despite our romanticism about the founding of our "democratic" country by noble and virtuous leaders, the fact is that many of the founders did not trust in democracy and therefore created a system in which only a privileged few would be in control. Many of the founders believed that the masses were corruptible and easily swayed by factions or demagogues. Madison expressed it this way: "the people, stimulated by some irregular passion, or some illicit advantage, or misled by the artful misrepresentations of interested men, may call for measures which they themselves will afterward be the most ready to lament and condemn." The founders' mistrust of the masses found its way into the Constitution, which restricted voting to only the privileged.

Not only did the founders deny women and non-whites the right to vote, but they also thought it advisable that qualified white men should meet certain requirements, most often based on net worth. They deemed wealth (e.g., landowning) as a sign that someone not only was smart and capable but also was hopefully beyond corruption because he was not economically vulnerable; the founders feared that poor people would sell their votes. Madison expressed the founders' concerns this way: "The right of suffrage is a fundamental Article in Republican Constitutions. The regulation of it is, at the same time, a task of peculiar delicacy. Allow the right [to vote] exclusively to property [owners], and the rights of persons may be oppressed … Extend it equally to all, and the rights of property [owners] … may be overruled by a majority without property." The founders erred on the side of protecting the wealthy and in the end created a republic (not democracy) that extended voting rights to a scant privileged 10 to 15 percent of the American population. The founders also left much discretion to the states in the voting process. For the first couple of decades after the Constitution's ratification, some states even restricted voting based on religious affiliation. Property requirements for voting were not fully repealed until more than half a century after the ratification of the Constitution. Remnants of the founders' cautions about the masses having the power to vote still exist today. None of us can directly vote for a presidential candidate; instead, we vote for electors to the Electoral College, who are duty-bound, but not actually required, to vote on our behalf for the candidate we chose. It is yet another buffer the founders put in place to limit the perceived dangers of direct democracy.

It was not until 1870 that the Fifteenth Amendment to the Constitution was passed, "prohibiting the federal and state governments from denying a citizen the right to vote based on that citizen's race, color, or previous condition of servitude." But as we know, that did not end efforts to discriminate based on race. Until the 1965 Voting Rights Act, many African Americans were precluded from voting in much of the South. Arizona and Maine prevented Native Americans from voting (despite their US citizenship) until the mid-twentieth century. And of course, prior to 1920, voting rights for women were partial in some places and denied altogether in much of the country. Immigrants have been subject to voting discrimination through much of our history. In the nineteenth century, many feared the ignorance of poor immigrants and tried to restrict their voting. In 1855, Connecticut introduced the first literacy test for American voters. In the next half century, the tests spread to almost all parts of the country. They helped many states in the South circumvent the Fifteenth Amendment and disenfranchise Blacks. Voter literacy tests were not permanently outlawed by Congress until 1975, years after the civil rights movement had discredited them.

After a long struggle for Women's Suffrage, it was 100 years ago on August 26, 1920 that the 19th Amendment was adopted as part the US Constitution giving American women the right to vote. It took forty-two years after the amendment was first introduced in Congress to get it enacted. The 19th Amendment extended the vote in theory to all women of voting age though it would be many decades until Black, Asian-American, and Native American women gained wide voting rights.

Here in the twenty-first century, we have inherited the broad voting rights that came about only after a long struggle. It took nearly two centuries for the nation to move toward a model approaching universal suffrage. But as far as we have come, we see states still trying to enact voter restrictions. There are fifteen states with relatively new voting laws that have never before been used during a presidential election, per a report by the Brennan Center for Justice. These laws include such restrictions as voter ID requirements (many of which selectively require documentation that tends to restrict minorities, students, the elderly, and the like) and limits on early voting. Several discriminatory state laws have been struck down in recent years, including those many consider the most blatantly racially inspired—that is, those of North Carolina and Texas. North Dakota's law was also struck down because of its potential impact on Native Americans. The court documents in the North Carolina case revealed blatant attempts by the state legislature to repress minority voting. E-mail exchanges revealed that key legislators knew that most African Americans in the state voted early (60 and 64 percent in 2008 and 2012, respectively, compared with 44 and 49 percent for whites), and so efforts were initiated to significantly restrict early voting. The legislature's research also showed that African Americans more often lacked driver's licenses, the most common form of voter ID, so the legislature intentionally formulated the law to remove other common forms of identification from the list of acceptable IDs, in order to further restrict minority voter eligibility. The final point that led the court to overturn the law was the fact that the state could show no voter fraud that would have prompted such laws. Fortunately, these most discriminatory provisions were reversed prior to the 2020 presidential election. Stacey Abrams, candidate for governor in Georgia in 2018, who faced questionable voter suppression efforts by her opponent, helped organize the Fair Fight PAC, which conducts programs to support voter protection programs at state parties around the country and is engaging in partnerships to support and elect progressive, pro–voting rights leaders. Stacey Abrams's says in her recent book, *Our Time is Now: Power, Purpose, and the Fight for a Fair America* that, "Over the course of our history, the right to vote had to be purchased by blood and protest in each generation" and she urges the nation to continue to fight for our fundamental right. It was her leadership in organizing voter turnout particularly among African Americans in 2020 that turned Georgia blue and elected Rev. Raphael Warnock, Georgia's first Black senator and the first Black Democrat to represent a southern state in the Senate along with Jon Ossoff, the first Jewish Senator from Georgia.

Further, we increasingly face another type of voter threat from social media disinformation campaigns, both foreign and domestic sources. McKay Coppins of the *Atlantic* spoke on NPR in mid-2020 about the Trump campaign's disinformation strategy for the 2020 elections, which he says could be the largest such campaign in US history. Coppins warned listeners to be skeptical of media sources they don't know; he advised voters to "seek out second and third sources to confirm, especially before you share it or make voting decisions based on it."

In 2020 another threat arrived in the form of the coronavirus. Some primaries had to be canceled, and greater use of mail-in ballots was permitted by most states despite unsupported attacks about mail ballot fraud from the political right including then President Trump. The Trump administration, in an apparent further effort to limit mail balloting, installed a political ally at the United States Postal Service who began reorganizing and cutting service in the months leading up to the 2020 elections. This triggered push back from Congress and many States resulting in an apparent Administration agreement to suspend changes until after the election. Still, without any proof, President Trump continually threatened during the 2020 campaign to not accept the election results because of massive illegal mail in ballots. Even after a convincing electoral college and popular vote defeat, Trump refused to concede and engaged in many frivolous state voting challenges as well as a social media campaign to undercut the election results. His campaign ultimately led to the violent and deadly invasion of the Capitol by white supremacists as legislators were acting to certify the election of Biden and Harris. This tragic fiasco is truly a stain on America's democratic history that will not be easily mitigated.

The right to vote is such a fundamental right in our country that we should be making extraordinary efforts to get everyone out to vote rather than implementing backdoor and discriminatory schemes to limit voters' opportunities to exercise their constitutional right. We have way too many who take our democracy for granted and do not even bother to show up at the polls. They use many excuses for not exercising their democratic right, with some even recently claiming that the system is massively rigged against their interests. We certainly do not have a perfect system, but as Winston Churchill suggested, democracy, even with its many imperfections, is better than all the other forms that have been tried over time.

Health Care

There is no specific guarantee of health care in our Constitution, but the Declaration of Independence states that all "men" have "unalienable Rights, that among these are Life, Liberty and the pursuit of Happiness," which would seem to imply having the health care needed to preserve life and pursue happiness. The World Health Organization states, "The enjoyment of the highest attainable standard of health is one of the fundamental rights of every human." Nevertheless, this issue gets continuing debate and resistance. Many presidents since Truman have pursued the idea of universal health care. President Johnson was instrumental in securing passage of Medicare, which covers all seniors sixty-five or older, and Medicaid, which provides health care for those in or just above the poverty level. President Obama and the Democratic-controlled Congress took a big step in 2010 with enactment of the Affordable Care Act (ACA), that sought to provide health coverage for all. According to the Centers for Disease Control, the medical uninsured rate in the US was down to almost 9 percent by 2015, as compared to around 16 percent before the Affordable Care Act was signed into law in 2010. The US Census Bureau reported that pre COVID in 2019, 8.0 percent of people, or 26.1 million, did not have health insurance at any point during the year. The Department of Health and Human Services also reported that since the ACA's coverage expansion began, over 20 million uninsured people nationwide gained health insurance coverage—the largest reduction in the uninsured in four decades. Despite that good news, we still have way too many uninsured Americans, in part because some twelve states still have declined to expand their Medicaid programs under provisions of the ACA, and these are largely southern states that have large minority populations with high uninsured rates. It is hard not to conclude from all this that there is also a racial element in some of the opposition to the ACA.

There have been some seventy Republican-led attempts to repeal, modify, or otherwise impede the ACA since its enactment in March 2010 including two unsuccessful cases before the Supreme Court. Now ten years later, Republican leaders still do not have a replacement plan, and many continue to attack the ACA and in fact are still trying to repeal it, even though upward of 20 million people could lose health coverage. The Trump Justice Department supported by some eighteen Republican attorneys general in going all the way to the Supreme Court again to invalidate the entire ACA because the individual mandate was removed by Congress in the 2017 tax overhaul. Although Congress did not disturb the remainder of the ACA, the state attorneys general and the Trump administration nevertheless went to the Supreme Court asking for total repeal, and of course there was never a replacement plan in sight. The suit, if successful, would end guaranteed coverage for people with preexisting conditions, an ACA benefit that Republicans say they strongly support.

When will the Republican cynicism on healthcare policy sink in with their core constituencies, many of whom rely on the ACA for health care including those with preexisting conditions? It seems that repealing Obamacare had been a party rallying cry, seemingly because the law was associated with former President Obama. In 2019, House Democrats passed a sensible bill to strengthen the ACA; it would have expanded federal insurance subsidies and reversed the Trump administration's attacks on the health care law while avoiding the more ambitious proposals to extend health coverage to all, but it never had a chance in the Republican controlled Senate. Now we look to a new President and a new Congress to take the next steps on healthcare reform in light of the nation's health tragedy from the COVID-19 pandemic.

This continuing spectacle is so sad, cynical, and ultimately threatening to millions throughout the country. What could be the possible motivation of a major political party to seek to deny so many Americans vital health coverage? For whatever reason, many Republican lawmakers seem to hate the idea of poor and working-class Americans getting the health care they need, even if their opposition hurts their own constituents. With the COVID-19 outbreak in 2020, the healthcare system is being tested beyond anything seen in years. Uncertainty will be part of the backdrop for the foreseeable future, and those without health coverage are more vulnerable than ever as we just witnessed a year of record deaths in 2020. Congress enacted temporary economic and health measures to cover those most affected by the pandemic, and this is likely to increase the pressure for more permanent solutions. Telemedicine is one of the growth stories of the COVID-19 pandemic and potentially offers hope for improved access to health services.

The more than fifty-year-old Medicare system is a good example of the process to follow for improving the ACA. Although Medicare largely accomplished its two key goals of ensuring access to health care for its 55 million senior and disabled beneficiaries and protecting them against the financial hardship of health care costs, Medicare has been modified with bipartisan enhancements many times over the years to better respond to the needs of seniors.

For lower-income individuals and families in poverty, Medicaid has been a lifeline, and it was expanded to 138 percent of the poverty line under the ACA, at states' option. Unfortunately, eighteen states did not expand Medicaid coverage under the ACA, and the number still stands at twelve states. In these states, over two million poor uninsured adults fall into the "coverage gap" that results from their states' decisions not to expand Medicaid, which leaves these residents also below the lower limit for ACA marketplace premium tax credits. Increasingly, conservative state legislatures are adding work requirements for Medicaid eligibility. Many think that putting such restrictions on basic health care is inhumane and argue that access to medical care is often a precursor to getting back to work, so the restriction is counterproductive to the desired outcome.

Democrats want a system that provides affordable and quality universal healthcare, but there is a divide on how to achieve that goal. Republicans, meanwhile, are lost in the wilderness on health care reform, having promised for years to offer an alternative with nothing to show. "Medicare for All" was proposed by Bernie Sanders of Vermont and Elizabeth Warren of Massachusetts among other liberal Democrats, a system where all Americans would be required to get insurance through the government. The proposal would eliminate private insurers as well as payments like premiums, copays, and deductibles. More moderate Democrats, including President Biden, are pushing for an expansion of the ACA through a public option, where Americans are given the option of buying into a single-payer system like Medicare. Several bills were introduced in the last Congress to make Medicare a public option, available to individuals and employers. These proposals, unlike Medicare for All, represent a gradual expansion of the ACA to eventually reach universal coverage. Importantly, the Bipartisan Policy Center recently released recommendations from its Future of Health Care initiative with a bipartisan group of leading national policy experts, led by Democrat Tom Daschle and Republican Bill Fritz, both former Senate majority leaders. The center endorses building on our current system's blend of public and private health care.[53] Its polling is consistent with that of other organizations, showing that Americans significantly prefer building on the current ACA-based system over either the liberal Medicare for All proposal or the repeal-and-replace Republican effort.

As in 2018, healthcare policy was again a key issue in the 2020 elections magnified by the COVID-19 pandemic. March 2020 was the tenth anniversary of passage of the ACA. Isn't it time to quit politically fighting about it (note: twenty state attorneys general and the Trump administration were at the Supreme Court to try to repeal the ACA during the COVID-19 pandemic!) and move as quickly as possible toward universal coverage? Trying to repeal the ACA in light of the vulnerabilities exposed by the coronavirus pandemic is insanity. And the fact that we still have twelve States (generally with poorer populations) that have not extended Medicaid benefits under the ACA to their citizens is tragic in light of the health crisis faced during the coronavirus pandemic. The new Biden Administration has comprehensive health proposals including enacting a public health insurance option and reducing the Medicare age to sixty as measures to move the country toward universal health coverage, but the divided political climate may preclude any comprehensive solutions in the near future.

Certainly, Trump's administrative rollbacks to the ACA will be reversed by the new Biden administration.

Gay Rights

In the US, there were few attempts to create advocacy groups supporting gay and lesbian relationships until after World War II. However, prewar gay life flourished in urban centers such as New York's Greenwich Village. The gay liberation movement began to emerge in the 1970s with a myriad of political organizations springing up. Perhaps the most important for the gay community was the 'Stonewall' uprising by members of the gay community in response to a police raid that began in the early morning hours of June 28, 1969, at the Stonewall Inn in the Greenwich Village neighborhood of Manhattan. Patrons of the Stonewall and other supporters fought back when the police became violent. Stonewall is widely considered to be one of the most important events leading to the gay liberation movement and the modern fight for LGBT rights in the U.S. Today Pride events are held annually throughout the world toward the end of June to mark the Stonewall riots. Stonewall 50 – WorldPride NYC in June 2019 commemorated the 50th anniversary of the Stonewall uprising with city officials and several million holding a massive rally in Manhattan. Also, on June 6, 2019, New York City Police Commissioner James P. O'Neill issued a formal apology on behalf of the New York Police Department for the actions of its officers at Stonewall in 1969.

Frustrated with the male leadership of most gay liberation groups, lesbians influenced by the feminist movement of the 1970s formed their own organizations and called for lesbian rights in mainstream feminist groups such as the National

Organization for Women. Importantly, in 1973, the American Psychiatric Association removed homosexuality from its list of mental disorders in the *Diagnostic and Statistical Manual of Mental Disorders* (*DSM-II*). From about 1988, activists began to use the initialism LGBT, but it was well into the 1990s before gay, lesbian, bisexual, and transgender people gained equal respect in the movement. "LGBT" has now expanded to "LGBTQ" in a growing number of circles, with the "Q" standing for "queer." Also becoming more prevalent is "LGBTQIA," where the "I" stands for "intersex" and the "A" for "asexual" and/or "allied."

In 1993, President Bill Clinton signed a military policy directive that prohibited openly gay and lesbian Americans from serving in the military but also prohibited the harassment of "closeted" homosexuals. The policy was known as "Don't Ask, Don't Tell." In 1996, the US Congress passed, and President Bill Clinton signed, the Defense of Marriage Act, a law that prohibited federal recognition of same-sex marriages. In 2003, Massachusetts judges ruled that the state constitution allowed gay marriage, and marriage licenses followed shortly after that. In reaction, several states banned same-sex marriage; such laws included Proposition 8 in California, which was subsequently overturned by the courts in 2010. "Freedom to Marry" activists in the last decade developed a smart approach to advocacy for same-sex marriage rights. They began an effort to personalize their campaign for LGBTQ people. They emphasized one-on-one relationships; they transitioned from a focus on discrimination to one of fundamental desire for everyone to have loving, caring relationships. They also trained supporters to each have personal conversations with five of their friends or relatives—and to ask people who responded positively to seek out five more. Momentum began to build. In 2011, "Don't Ask,

Don't Tell" was repealed, ending a ban on gay men and lesbians serving openly in the military.

The June 2013 decision of the US Supreme Court, in *United States v. Windsor*, striking down the law barring federal recognition of same-sex marriage, gave significant impetus to the progress of lawsuits that challenged state bans on same-sex marriage in federal court. A critical turning point came in October 2014, when the Supreme Court chose not to hear appeals against lower court rulings that had overturned same-sex marriage bans—expanding the legality of same-sex unions to many more states. On June 26, 2015, the US Supreme Court struck down all state bans on same-sex marriage, legalized it in all fifty states, and required states to honor out-of-state same-sex marriage licenses in the case *Obergefell v. Hodges*. Since the US Supreme Court ruling, support for same-sex marriage has increased substantially. According to a large PRRI survey conducted in April–December 2017, the issue of same-sex marriage has broad consensus among young adults (ages eighteen to twenty-nine).[54] The results showed that more than three-quarters (77 percent) favored legalization of same-sex marriage, including nearly half (45 percent) who strongly favored it, while only 17 percent of young adults were opposed. In contrast, the study showed that fewer than half (47 percent) of seniors (ages sixty-five and up) thought same-sex marriage should be legal, while about four in ten (42 percent) opposed it.

The PRRI study showed that partisan gaps in views of same-sex marriage persist, however. Nearly three-quarters of Democrats and about two-thirds of independents favored same-sex marriage, compared to only 42 percent of Republicans. A slim majority of Republicans opposed same-sex marriage, with opposition occurring mostly among more conservative Republicans. Regarding religious groups' attitudes, majorities of nearly every major religious group supported legal protection against discrimination for LGBTQ Americans. Results showed that 60 percent of Americans oppose allowing small business owners in their state to refuse service to gay and lesbian people if doing so would violate their religious beliefs, while just one-third of Americans supported allowing such businesses to refuse service to LGBTQ. Importantly, in June 2020, the Supreme Court ruled that the 1964 civil rights law protects gay and transgender workers from workplace discrimination. Before this decision, it was legal in more than half of the states to fire workers for being gay, bisexual, or transgender. This hugely consequential decision extended full workplace protections to millions of people across the nation and notably came during Pride Month.

Support for same-sex marriage should be embraced even more widely because of the societal benefits of two-parent families. Researchers Sara McLanahan and Isabel Sawhill note in their 2015 report *Future of Children* that "most scholars now agree that children raised by two parents in a stable marriage do better than children in other family forms across a wide variety of outcomes." The 2015 Supreme Court majority opinion in favor of national same-sex marriage rights said that marriage is a key building block of our national community and ruled that that right should be available to gay couples as well. Their opinion found no basis for the argument that same-sex marriage would have a detrimental effect on the institution of marriage. In fact, many believe it expands and strengthens the institution of marriage, which has been on the decline. My church has long been welcoming of gay and lesbian persons and families and has been so enriched by their presence. The idea that their marriages and family presence among us somehow threatens my traditional marriage seems ludicrous. "Family values" conservatives and progressives should be able to come together in support of marriage regardless of what form it takes because of the positive benefits for families, children, and society.

Immigration

Immigration has been a contentious issue through much of our country's history, even though Americans today are mostly descended from immigrants. The first significant federal legislation restricting immigration was the 1882 Chinese Exclusion Act, in reaction to significant Chinese labor being used to build the transcontinental railroad. In the following decade, the Immigration Restriction League was formed around the emerging science of eugenics. Founded in 1894 by three recent Harvard University graduates, the league sought to bar what it considered inferior races from entering America and diluting what it saw as the superior American racial stock (of Anglo-Saxon heritage). The league lobbied for a literacy test for immigrants, based on the belief that literacy rates were low among "inferior races." Literacy test bills were vetoed by presidents in 1897, 1913, and 1915; eventually, President Wilson's second veto was overruled by Congress in 1917. This led to passage of the Immigration Act of 1924, where eugenicists played an important role in the congressional debate as expert advisers on the threat of "inferior stock" coming to America, particularly from eastern and southern Europe. The act, built on the eugenic belief in the racial superiority of white "Nordic" European Americans, also helped solidify existing laws prohibiting race-mixing. Immigration levels fell during the Depression years, but following World War II, labor demand increased, and pressure to open up immigration gradually emerged. In 1965, Congress passed the Immigration and Nationality Act, which did away with quotas based on nationality, primarily focused on western Europe. This resulted in more Asian and Latin American immigrants and other people of color and the specter of the US becoming a minority population in coming decades. This "scare" is spurring pressures for more immigration restrictions.

History shows that immigration has boosted US economic growth and still does today. The Kauffman Foundation's Index of Startup Activity in 2016 showed that immigrants were almost twice as likely as native-born Americans to start new businesses in the United States. A report from the Partnership for a New American Economy found that in 2016, 40 percent of Fortune 500 firms had "at least one founder who either immigrated to the United States or was the child of immigrants." There is a global competition for workers, including highly skilled workers to develop new technologies and lower-skilled workers to support agriculture. This is a competition America has benefited from decade after decade, and we will need it more in future years since our native population growth is slowing. We will need more immigrant workers to fill that gap. Some immigration opponents fear that immigrants could displace native-born American workers, but most economic research on this issue shows that immigration has historically led to faster overall growth and a higher per capita standard of living.

If political leaders could only agree on fixes to our immigration system to ensure a continuing legal flow of needed new workers, it could be a big benefit to our economy. The Minneapolis Federal Reserve estimates that our economic growth could increase by at least half a percentage point per year with a well-tailored immigration policy. With the support of the Obama administration in 2013, a big majority of Democrats and Republicans came together in the Senate to pass a comprehensive bipartisan immigration reform bill that would have improved border security and fixed many of the issues with today's immigration process. It would have given law-abiding undocumented immigrants and their families a path to permanent legal residence. It also shifted the country's immigration policies more toward immigrants who could bring our country's needed work skills. All the major interest groups—from government, business, labor, social justice organizations, and the like—supported the bill. It would have solved so many of the immigration issues that have been lingering and festering for years. The immigration programs in Canada and Australia are more skills-based than the US system currently, more like what the Senate bill would have created in 2013. Most immigrants to Canada and Australia come from developing countries, the largest being India and China, followed by the Philippines, countries whose emigrants have many skills that Canada and Australia need for their growing economies.

Unfortunately, in 2013, House "Tea Party" members prevented the Senate immigration bill from coming to the House floor, and the effort failed. The issued got kicked down the road and became a lightning rod in the 2016 presidential campaign. Donald Trump ran on a rabid anti-immigrant campaign, at one-point saying:

> When Mexico sends its people, they're not sending their best … They're bringing drugs. They're bringing crime. They're rapists. And some, I assume, are good people. It's coming from more than Mexico. It's coming from all South and Latin America, and it's coming, probably, probably, from the Middle East. But we don't know, because we have no protection, and we have no competence, and we don't know what's happening.

After the Trump administration took office in January 2017, it initiated an aggressive plan to go after illegal immigration, warning that all the estimated 11 million undocumented immigrants currently living in the United States were subject to deportation at any time. Trump's initial executive order on immigration supposedly targeted criminals as its top priority, but the language was so broad that it could include almost anyone in the country without legal status. Thousands of families have been and are being affected, the typical case being citizen children with one or both parents undocumented. Per Pew Research, most people living in the US illegally have been here for a long time, are working in agricultural, fast food, and home service jobs, and are contributing to the US economy and paying taxes. Two-thirds have been in the US a decade or more, according to Pew's analysis. under 15 percent have been here less than five years. Instead of immigration reform, we saw the Trump administration pursuing a massive deportation approach that in many cases broke up families who have been here many years and who were contributing positively to the US economy. Further, the administration drastically lowered the number of refugees allowed into the country at a time when the world has a record number of refugees, many of whom have been victims of wars our country is engaged in. The Trump administration-built walls literally and figuratively, and in many cases it was against the country's economic interests. Waiting times for visas, work permits, and green cards (including for much-needed skilled workers such as H1b applicants) increased from six months to a year or more.

Faith communities went into action to help families caught up in these chaotic immigration policies. My church in DC has been engaged with the Latino community in the neighborhood around the church near Thomas Circle for several years and has gotten to know the precarious situations of many immigrant families. My church is currently engaged with other DC-area congregations in a metropolitan-wide organization called the Congregation Action Network that is fighting on behalf of threatened immigrants, including through legislative advocacy, legal assistance, accompaniment to immigration hearings, and sanctuary. Our congregation previously provided sanctuary in the 1980s to Central American refugees who were escaping violence in their home countries.

Sanctuary has religious roots in the Judeo-Christian tradition. In the Old Testament, God commanded Moses to set aside cities and places of refuge in Canaan where the persecuted could seek asylum. Those ideas have been embraced by historical movements, from the Underground Railroad during slavery in the US to efforts to provide sanctuary to Jews during World War II. But it was during the 1980s that a large sanctuary movement was launched in this country, led by the faith community. At the time, there were refugees arriving as a result of violent crackdowns by dictators (often supported by the US government) in Central America. The policy of the Reagan administration was primarily to detain and deport those who sought asylum from those regimes. As a result, churches opened their doors to provide shelter and support—and denied entry to federal officials. The election of Donald Trump and his mass deportation rhetoric reignited the sanctuary movement. The rhetoric and the significantly increased deportation in the Trump administration greatly increased fear among unauthorized immigrant families and children. Families were torn apart when undocumented parents were deported, often leaving citizen children behind; it is estimated that four to five million US citizen children have at least one parent who is undocumented.

After months of indecision, in September 2017, the Trump administration announced the end (by March 7, 2018, if Congress didn't act) of the Deferred Action for Childhood Arrivals (DACA) program started by President Obama in 2012, which allowed young unauthorized immigrants (Dreamers) who had been brought to the US as children to apply for temporary protection from deportation and work permits. The March 7 date passed without congressional action, but the federal courts intervened and required the administration to continue processing Dreamer applications for work permits. The Obama administration created the DACA program in 2012, in response to repeated failures by Congress to create a permanent path to legal status for people who were brought to the US as children through no action of their own. Many have lived in the US almost their entire lives and have gone to school here, many to college, and some have US citizen spouses and children. Typically, the US is the only country they consider home. Nearly 800,000 young people have received DACA status, and an estimated 1.1 million are eligible. The DACA program has had a tremendous impact on the lives of its recipients and their communities, enabling thousands of them to pursue education and careers and contribute billions of dollars to the US economy.

A study by the Center for American Progress showed that nearly half of Dreamers are currently in school. Of these individuals, over 80 percent were found to be working. Among those who are currently in school, 70 percent are pursuing a bachelor's degree. Importantly, among those who are currently in school, over 90 percent said that because of DACA, they had pursued educational opportunities that they previously could not. Meanwhile, these young people are facing great uncertainty and fear. Jasmine L. Tyler, US advocacy director at Human Rights Watch, says, "Trump's repeal of DACA ... exposes hundreds of thousands of people to deportation by a cruel and unjust immigration system that fails to take into account their deep ties to the US." Meanwhile, many faith groups around the country are offering support, including sanctuary if necessary. The DC metro area's Congregation Action Network has been supporting DACA advocates who come into town to protest at the White House and Capitol Hill. My church housed many of the DACA protest groups in its Steinbruck Center hostel. June 15, 2020 was the eight-year anniversary since the implementation of DACA. Clearly, it is time for a permanent solution!

In mid-2018, the Trump administration announced that when families arrive at the border for asylum, officials would separate children from their parents. It has been widely reported that between October 1, 2017, and May 31, 2018, at least 2,700 immigrant children of families seeking refuge were split from their parents. Liz Goodwin, a reporter for the *Boston Globe*, tweeted that a public defender in McAllen said that "some migrants are told their kids are going to be taken away briefly to bathe, and then it dawns on them hours later they aren't coming back." This stirs tragic memories of another era when such language was used as families were separated upon arrival at the concentration camps! And unfortunately, this cruelty of separating families is not new in our own history—we separated children from their mothers during the slave trade and separated Native American families. It is intolerable that this is happening again. The UN Human Rights Office called for an immediate halt to this administration's heartless policy. The American Academy of Pediatrics also offered condemnation, warning of the potential long-term effects and that trauma inflicted on these children would affect their physical and emotional health and could have dire lifelong consequences.

The administration even claimed a divine right to separate

children and send them off to warehouses. Then attorney general Jeff Sessions claimed that the Bible justified this treatment, referring to Romans 13, where it advises people to submit to the authorities. But this ignores the context of what comes before and after that reference: "share with the Lord's people who are in need … Practice hospitality" and "love each other; for the one who loves another has fulfilled the law." Even evangelical leaders who have fully embraced the administration's policies spoke out on this issue. The Catholic Conference of Bishops said at the time,

> At its core, asylum is an instrument to preserve the right to life. The attorney general's recent decision elicits deep concerns, because it potentially strips asylum for many women who lack adequate protection … While protecting our borders is important, we can and we … must do better as a government and as a society to find other ways to ensure that safety. Separating babies from their mothers is not the answer and is immoral.

This is the kind of policy that emerges when immigrants are dehumanized, called animals, and worse. Medical experts suggest that such separation can inflict enormous trauma on children. In an ACLU lawsuit over the separation of families in immigration detention, a Department of Justice official told the judge that "once a parent is in ICE [Immigration and Customs Enforcement] custody and the child is taken into the Health and Human Services system, the government does not try to reunite them, and instead attempts to place the child with another relative in the United States—if the child has one." ICE and the Department of Homeland Security, however, claimed that once parents have finished their criminal sentences for illegal entry or reentry, they can be reunited with their children in civil immigration detention while they pursue their asylum case. Most experts concluded that the Trump administration really did not have an effective system to bring families back together and only recently we learned there are still some 545 separated children stuck in our immigration system in late 2020. Seen here is a picture of a Congregation Action Network interfaith protest in the Senate Russell Building Rotunda on June 21, 2018, to push Congress to restrict the Trump administration's harsh family separation and detention policies at the border. Children at the protest were wrapped in aluminum foil–type blankets, in reference to those often used by ICE at the border.

Congregation Action Network interfaith protest in the
Senate Russell Building Rotunda on June 21, 2018

We have a humanitarian crisis around immigration, but it is not resolved through demeaning treatment of people who are desperate for a better life. Children are often the victims of the haphazard and cruel immigration policies of this administration. Many hundreds of children have been and are being held in the custody of US Border Patrol without their parents. Legally, they are not supposed to be held by border agents for than seventy-two hours before being sent to the Department of Health and Human Services, which is responsible for finding their nearest relative in the US to house them while their immigration cases are adjudicated. In practice, they have been held for days, sometimes weeks, in overcrowded conditions, often without enough food and without proper hygiene and medical care.

In a key action at its 2019 Churchwide Assembly, the Evangelical Lutheran Church of America voted to approve a memorial that declares the ELCA a sanctuary church. My Luther Place congregation in downtown DC is part of the ELCA. This is the first North American denomination to declare itself a sanctuary church body. As a sanctuary church, the ELCA is committed to serving and supporting migrant children and families in communities across the country. The Rev. Elizabeth Eaton, presiding bishop of the ELCA, joined more than seven hundred assembly members and others in a march and prayer vigil to the Milwaukee ICE office during the assembly. The ELCA Milwaukee Synod Refuge and Immigration Committee said in conjunction with the national ELCA event, "We firmly believe that the treatment of children and families in our border is a moral issue, not a political one. The well-being and safety of children, including ensuring family unity and reunification, must be a priority. Therefore, we commit ourselves to an ongoing struggle for just immigration policies."

"Give me your tired, your poor, your huddled masses yearning to breathe free," reads the marker on the Statue of Liberty, which was a welcoming symbol to many millions of refugees and immigrants coming into Ellis Island over the last centuries. In an interview in August 2019, the Trump administration's top immigration official, Ken Cuccinelli, acting director of US Citizenship and Immigration Services, essentially refuted this widely embraced motto, saying we will embrace only immigrants who can "stand on their own two feet" and "not become a public charge." In a subsequent interview, he went a step further, saying the motto referred to "people coming from Europe"—which, of course, is code for "whites only." His comments came a day after the administration announced a new rule rejecting green cards for immigrants who might rely on any kind of government assistance. The president himself continually spoke disparagingly about immigrants from majority Black and Hispanic countries, including calling Mexican immigrants rapists and criminals when he launched his 2016 campaign, and he frequently cited refugees arriving at our borders as "an invasion."

Surveys show that most Americans want a few basic things in our immigration policy: fair and compassionate treatment of immigrants; a path to citizenship for those here long-term and working or being educated, such as the Dreamers and Temporary Protected Status (TPS) recipients; and finally, improved security at our borders. This broad consensus unfortunately gets lost in the current highly charged political debate.

Meanwhile, we should help build better police and justice systems in the home countries of refugees from Central America. Rather than cutting aid to Central American countries as the administration did, we need sustained efforts to help reduce crime, improve governance, and facilitate economic growth, particularly in El Salvador, Honduras, and Guatemala. The US successfully worked with Colombia to achieve a similar outcome in the last two decades, so we know it is possible.

Looking at other Western countries' immigration systems suggests three main elements to effective immigration programs: an economic component, a family component, and a humanitarian component. Canada, for example, takes in many more immigrants proportionally than the United States and makes notably more effort to integrate them into society. Canada takes in about the same number of family-based immigrants but many more skill-based immigrants than we do. It does a much better job of assessing skill-based needs nationally and in the provinces and then adjusts its immigration targets each year to meet those job needs. It also accommodates temporary workers and refugees. There is clearly a path forward and seemingly a broad public consensus about the key parts of a compromise; unfortunately, our broken political process stands in the way.

The House importantly made a start toward reform with passage of the American Dream and Promise Act of 2019, a bill that would offer a path to citizenship to more than two million undocumented immigrants, including Dreamers who were brought to the United States as children. In addition to Dreamers, the House bill would offer protections to TPS holders, which has allowed people from El Salvador, Haiti, Honduras, and other countries to avoid being deported to nations engulfed in war or affected by natural disasters. In November 2019, the administration's DACA rescission went before the Supreme Court for debate, with a decision in June 2020 against the Administration's inadequately supported recission but allowing for resubmission. Clearly, the Dreamers and TPS holders must be protected and offered an eventual path toward citizenship. Now in 2021, the incoming Biden Administration on its first day launched a series of executive orders to reverse the damage of the Trump Administration and submitted a comprehensive immigration reform bill to Congress.

Right to Universal Education

Much to the surprise of most Americans, the US Constitution, including its amendments, makes no explicit reference to education or the right of citizens to education. It thus falls to state and local governments to determine the amount of education and right to that education for their citizenry. The Constitution does require that all be given equal educational opportunity, no matter their race, ethnic background, religion, or sex, or whether they are rich or poor, citizen or non-citizen. In addition to this constitutional guarantee of an equal opportunity, many federal, state, and local laws also protect students against discrimination in education based on sexual orientation or disability, including pregnancy and HIV status. The Supreme Court importantly spoke to educational discrimination in the landmark 1954 case *Brown v. Board of Education*, when it struck down racial segregation in public schools. But that did not necessarily lead to equal education. White students whose families had resources often fled to private schools, leaving poorer students behind. A key problem of public education funded at the local level is that such systems rely heavily on local property taxes. Property values vary greatly from neighborhood to neighborhood and district to district, and so do the tax revenues for schools. Poorer neighborhoods are thus at a distinct disadvantage. To help poorer schools compensate for that local imbalance, some states have stepped in to increase efforts to equalize education spending, enforce higher teaching standards, and reduce teacher shortages; Connecticut, Kentucky, Minnesota, and North

Carolina are key examples. The closing of schools during the COVID-19 pandemic and the quick switch to distance learning has further laid bare the persistent inequities in educational opportunities that exist across the country. Unlike low-income students, children from middle-class and affluent households almost all have Internet access at home, as well as web-enabled devices. They also have plenty of books and other resources to get them through the crisis unlike poor children. Kids in low-income families are also missing their school lunches, so hunger and nutrition challenges have become more widespread.

Prekindergarten educational opportunity, such as that provided by Head Start, has been an important issue in recent years. After years of debate, some of the nation's top researchers have conclusively found that kids who attend public preschool programs are better prepared for kindergarten than kids who do not. The findings are found in a report titled *The Current State of Scientific Knowledge on Pre-Kindergarten Effects*, and the authors include big names from the early childhood world, including Deborah Phillips of Georgetown University, Mark W. Lipsey of Vanderbilt, Kenneth Dodge of Duke, Ron Haskins of the Brookings Institution, and others. The report lays out the current state of preschool education in the US and what research can tell us about what works and what does not. One of the key findings is that although all kids benefit from preschool, poor and disadvantaged kids often make the most gains. Supporters of publicly funded preschool for all children cite research that shows significant long-term benefits for children who attend preschool, including improved health, social, and behavioral outcomes, as well as higher income than the control group.

Funding continues to be an issue for the public school system and the COVID-19 pandemic only worsens the situation for state and local government education budgets; the Center on

Budget and Policy Priorities found in 2017 that thirty-four states were contributing less funding on a per-student basis than they did prior to the Great Recession. The National Assessment of Educational Progress, the largest standardized test administered in the United States, reports that fewer than 40 percent of graduating seniors have mastered reading and math, and they are poorly equipped for college and real-world life.

Our economy clearly favors those with education and vocational training after high school and punishes those who lack it. We need more access to and success in higher education, and we especially need it for the people who have consistently been left behind; low-income and first-generation students, students of color, and working adults. The Democratic 2020 platform proposed free college or vocational tuition for lower income students. Something clearly must be done, given that private college tuition and fees in the more elite schools has reached $75,000 or more per year; state universities have gotten much more expensive also as states have cut back funding. The large postsecondary education debt incurred by so many young people in recent decades is not a sustainable model for the future. A number of education experts are suggesting that faster, cheaper, specialized education and training are needed going forward that more closely aligns with labor markets and is updated incrementally over a lifetime of work.

More emphasis on community college is needed, with a focus on training for the emerging workplace; this presumably would be done in close collaboration with industries in the college's region. Google recently announced a program that could help change higher education and job training for many if the trend catches on with other companies. Google is launching a selection of professional courses that teach candidates how to perform in higher demand technical jobs. These courses, which the company is calling Google Career Certificates, teach foundational skills that can help jobseekers immediately find employment. And unlike college, it only takes about six months and is relatively inexpensive.

Americans with Disabilities

The Americans With Disabilities Act (ADA) was passed thirty years ago and was signed into law by President George H.W. Bush with wide bipartisan support. It was a major turning point in opening large parts of US society to disabled people. It prohibited discrimination against people with disabilities in areas such as employment, transportation, and public accommodations. It is estimated that one of every five Americans has a disability. In 2008, the ADA Amendments Act was passed to provide a more inclusive definition of impairment, which more accurately reflects the natural history of many chronic illnesses. The ability for the disabled to participate in the mainstream of society has gradually increased during the last 30 years but some issues still remain particularly in regard to workplace accommodation. The Centers for Disease Control and Prevention (CDC) reports that 61 million Americans are living with a disability. Persons with disabilities are at higher risk of unemployment, health conditions such as cardiovascular disease and obesity, as well as having less access to medical care. With greater employment gaps, disabled persons generally have lower income and access to affordable and safe housing. Also, race often contributes to even greater disparities in economic and health status of those with disabilities.

Safety and Security

In a post-9/11 environment, public safety and security concerns have been elevated in the public consciousness. After 9/11, we initiated wars on terrorism on multiple fronts in the Middle East with seemingly no end in sight. Although international terrorism gets the most political attention, our biggest challenge really is domestic terrorism and violence. According to a recent report by the nonpartisan Stimson Center, between 2002 and 2017, the United States spent $2.8 trillion on international counterterrorism. The center reports that terrorist attacks by Muslim extremists killed one hundred people in the United States during that time. But between 2008 and 2017, domestic extremists killed 387 in the US, according to a 2018 Anti-Defamation League report. In recent years, the Anti-Defamation League finds that white supremacist and anti-Semitic incidents have increased dramatically. As mentioned previously, the mid-2017 Charlottesville protests over dismantling Confederate monuments are just one example of white nationalist rallies featuring hate speech and violence, including the death of a young woman at the hands of a white nationalist. Three Black churches were set on fire in April 2019 in Louisiana, and a white man was charged with hate crimes. Anti-Semitism is on the rise, as exemplified by the killing of eleven Jewish worshippers at the Tree of Life Synagogue in Pittsburgh in October 2018 and the May 2019 synagogue attack near San Diego, California, where one congregant was killed. Personal attacks motivated by bias or prejudice reached a sixteen-year high in 2018, according to FBI reporting, with a particular upswing in violence against Latinos. A tragic example of the targeting of Latino immigrants was the August 2019 mass shooting at a Walmart store in El Paso, Texas, where the gunman shot and killed twenty-two people and injured twenty-four others.

Tragically, school shootings have become routine in the United States. Since the Columbine school shootings in 1999, its estimated that more than 228,000 children at 234 primary and secondary schools have experienced a shooting on campus during school hours, according to a recent *Washington Post* analysis. How can we accept this as a norm for our nation's children?

In its 2017 health tracking poll, the Kaiser Family Foundation surveyed more than 1,200 adults on several issues, including what worried them the most. Surprisingly and sadly, 42 percent of respondents said they were either somewhat worried or very worried about being the victim of gun violence. That is a higher share than those who were worried about losing their jobs, about being able to pay their rent or mortgage, or about being the victim of a terrorist attack. The November 2017 mass killing at the First Baptist Church in Sutherland, Texas, by an angry white male known to be an animal torturer and wife and child abuser, in the church his former wife's parents occasionally attended, is unfortunately the most common type of mass killing in the United States. A significant share of gun violence in America is driven by domestic violence, and these shooters often kill bystanders along with family members. Research by Everytown for Gun Safety finds that in 57 percent of the mass shootings between January 2009 and June 2014, the perpetrator killed an intimate partner or family member, often with other "collateral" killings. Abusers intent on killing an intimate partner, especially if they use a gun, often take-out other people who happen to be on the scene—children, friends, grandparents, and total strangers—like the situation in Sutherland, where the abuser was looking to take out his wife's family members and all bystanders. While the stats show that guns are used to kill women in 53 percent of intimate partner homicides, they are responsible for 70 percent of the collateral victims. Further, domestic violence incidents are among the most lethal scenarios for police officers. The Everytown for Gun Safety report examined police deaths in the line of duty from 2010 through 2014 and found that domestic dispute calls led to more fatalities than any other kind of emergency call.

There has been, on average, a mass shooting nearly every day in America since the Sandy Hook massacre in December 2012, totaling more than 1,500 and counting. We often blame this on mental illness, yet no other industrialized nation has this problem, and surely, they have as many "sociopaths," per capita, as America. It is rather the wide-open availability of mass killing weapons that enables anger-filled men to perpetrate these shootings on their family members and innocent bystanders day after day in America.

The further sad part of all this—and further reason that it should be a family-values issues—is the impact on children. According to a recent study by the National Center for Injury Prevention and Control of the US Centers for Disease Control and Prevention (CDC) titled *Childhood Firearm Injuries in the United States*, nearly 1,300 children are killed and nearly 6,000 injured every year by firearms, and this may be an underestimate because of potential underreporting.[55] A *New York Times* review of hundreds of firearm deaths of children found that accidental shootings occurred roughly twice as often as the records indicate, because of idiosyncrasies in how such deaths are classified by the authorities. The annual totals of child firearm deaths and injuries reported by the CDC suggest there are more than three children killed per day and more than fifteen children treated per day for gunshot wounds. The CDC study reports that rates of firearm homicide among children are higher in many southern states and parts of the Midwest relative to other parts of the country. The study also reported, "Firearm homicides of younger children often … involved intimate partner or family conflict; older children more often died in the context of crime and violence … The shooter playing with a gun was the most common circumstance surrounding unintentional firearm deaths of both younger and older children." The study concludes that "pediatric firearm injuries and deaths are an important public health problem in the United States, contributing substantially each year to premature death, illness, and disability of children." The *American Journal of Medicine* reports that of twenty-two countries in the developed world, 91 percent of children under fourteen who died by gun violence in all these countries were in the United States! Yet in the United States, the response after major shootings is often to loosen restrictions on guns so we can supposedly better protect ourselves and our families. Unfortunately, we know that having a gun in the house greatly increases the chances of gun deaths or injuries, too often to children in the household. Disturbingly, many states have not adopted stronger laws to prevent children from accessing unsecured guns because of pressure from the gun lobby.

The simplest and most effective way to protect the home from intruders is a burglar alarm system. These systems further protect homes when residents are away by detecting both intruders and unintended fires. And the big advantage is that there are no accidental killings, which happen daily in America. It is a true national tragedy when we witness nearly 40,000-gun deaths and upward of 75,000 injuries per year (as of 2017), most often perpetrated on spouses, children, other family members, and bystanders. How is it that we so greatly fear international terrorism when every day the threat of violence in our communities is really what we should be concerned about? Protecting families from gun violence should be an easy issue for all Americans to rally around. Yet mass killings, often with military-style weapons that no self-respecting hunter would ever use, are a daily occurrence in America, while our leaders can only offer their "thoughts and prayers" for the daily family victims.

In my state, Maryland, our Republican governor Larry Hogan signed three new gun regulations into law in 2018, including a ban on so-called bump stocks. Another provision, extreme risk protection orders, allows family members to ask a judge to order the seizure of a gun from a person believed to be planning to hurt himself or herself or someone else. Sometimes referred to as "red flag" laws, these bills emerged in the wake of the mass shooting at Marjory Stoneman Douglas High School in Parkland, Florida. The Maryland governor also signed legislation requiring convicted domestic abusers to surrender guns to law enforcement or a firearms dealer. Governor Hogan described the three bills as "commonsense bipartisan measures that will keep guns out of the hands of the mentally ill and those with criminal backgrounds."

These measures add to provisions enacted by Maryland after the tragic Sandy Hook Elementary School mass shooting in December 2012. In early 2013, Maryland enacted a ban on new purchases of assault weapons, a ten-bullet limit on magazines, and requirements that handgun buyers undergo fingerprinting and target training. The Maryland bill also included restrictions on purchases by people with mental illness, barring anyone who has been involuntarily committed for mental health treatment from buying a gun. None of these laws affect legitimate uses of a wide range of guns for hunting and home or personal protection in our state. The laws are also supported by law enforcement officials in Maryland. In 2017, the Supreme Court turned away an appeal challenging Maryland's ban on assault weapons, which have been used in recent mass shootings, so Maryland law stands and can be a model for other states. Such widely supported gun safety measures are not a threat to the Second Amendment as many opponents claim.

The Johns Hopkins Center for Gun Policy and Research has studied the effect of state "permit-to-purchase laws."[56] The center examined data in Connecticut, which enacted a gun licensing law in 1995, and Missouri, which repealed a similar measure in 2007. In Connecticut, gun-related homicides dropped 40 percent over the next decade, while non-firearm homicides remained unchanged, according to the researchers. In Missouri, researchers found a 25 percent increase in firearm homicides and a 14 percent increase in overall killings over the five years after that state's repeal of licensing and background check requirements. Further, a project at the Boston University School of Public Health, which tracks dozens of different provisions of gun laws in the fifty states, primarily using Centers for Disease Control data, found that the relationship between gun laws and firearms deaths is compelling. In states like Alabama, Alaska, and Louisiana, where guns are lightly regulated, the rate of deaths by firearms (per 100,000 people) is more than four times higher than in New York, Connecticut, Hawaii, Massachusetts, and my state, Maryland, which have all enacted stricter gun laws.

In 2018, following the Parkland, Florida, school shooting, we saw mass youth movements protesting gun violence and calling for stricter controls. On March 24, 2018, demonstrators flooded streets across the globe in public protests calling for action against gun violence. Hundreds of thousands of marchers turned out, in the most amazing show of force yet from the student-driven movement that emerged after the Parkland shooting. The mass student demonstrations helped ensure enactment of Maryland's new laws mentioned earlier. Even the permissive gun state of Florida was moved by student pressure to enact restrictions on assault weapons, among other measures. Let us hope this momentum continues. Gun reform could be the cause of this generation of young people, but only time will tell; let us hope they are more successful than their parents' generation has been.

There was a small bit of good news in that the US House of Representatives in 2019 passed its first gun measure (expanding background checks) in twenty-five years by a 240-to-190 bipartisan vote; it is now time to demand that the Senate take up this or similar gun safety measures. Former congresswoman Gabby Giffords, who nearly died from injuries inflicted by a gun assailant, said after the vote that stopping gun violence takes "courage … I have seen great courage when my life was on the line. Now is the time to come together, be responsible. Democrats, Republicans, everyone."

There was on average a mass shooting every day (gun incident involving at least four fatal or nonfatal injuries) in 2019. And it is clear this is a homegrown problem, not one of international terrorists or immigrant invaders! White supremacists are an increasing factor in high-visibility mass shootings. At a congressional hearing in May 2019, the head of the FBI's counterterrorism division testified that the bureau was investigating 850 domestic terrorism cases, and of those, about 40 percent involved racially motivated violent extremists, most of whom were white supremacists. Yet we had President Trump refusing to speak against white supremacists and in fact encouraging them by his incendiary language against BLM protestors in 2020.

Past political movements like the one against drunk driving (Mothers Against Drunk Driving) were successful because they tapped into deeper concerns about public safety and tapped an identity (e.g., mothers). This seems to also be the strategy behind Moms Demand Action for Gun Sense in America, which was formed after the Sandy Hook school shooting and which gained 50,000 new members following the Parkland School shooting. Other gun safety groups, including Everytown for Gun Safety, the Brady Campaign, Americans for Responsible Solutions, and the student led March for Our Lives are active in the current political environment and need support for enactment of sensible gun safety measures.

7

Environmental Sustainability

After several million years of evolution, humans in a matter of a few hundred years have rapidly elevated concerns about survival of our species and the planet as we know it. In the last one hundred years alone, the earth's climate has warmed about 1°C (1.8°F). As the climate has warmed, sea levels have been rising about one to two millimeters per year due to the reduction in volume of ice caps, ice fields, and mountain glaciers, in addition to the thermal expansion of ocean water. If present trends continue, including an increase in global temperatures caused by increased greenhouse gas emissions, many of the world's mountain glaciers will disappear. If warming continues at present rates, it is estimated that Iceland's glaciers will decrease by 40 percent by 2100 and virtually disappear by 2200. The real threat is in Antarctica, which has about 90 percent of the earth's polar ice sheet, and the Argentina national meteorological service reported a record temperature there in February 2020.

Homo sapiens have already survived some dramatic climate changes in their more than 200,000 years on Planet Earth and have seen some very rapid climate changes, but early humans were mobile and adaptable and so survived. The Holocene interglacial period began about 10,000 years ago, and it has proven to be a relatively stable environment on the earth. This stability and resilience have allowed agriculture to develop and complex societies to thrive. But since the Industrial Revolution, most scientists believe the planet has entered a new epoch, the Anthropocene, in which humans have become the main agents of change for the planet, and it is increasingly proving destructive. For example, notable scientists estimate that since the Anthropocene, the rate at which species are being extinguished has increased over one hundred times, and half the trees on the planet have been cut down for agriculture. In this period, humans have built major cities, and we now have at least a billion people living in threatened coastal regions, so the price of inaction is potentially very high.

We can and should slow down our carbon dioxide emissions, which are accelerating climate warming and sea level rise concurrent with natural warming in this interglacial period. We cannot precisely calculate the relative contribution of natural interglacial warming versus human-caused warming, but clearly, carbon dioxide levels have increased dramatically since the Industrial Revolution and now exceed 400 parts per million (ppm), the highest in more than 800,000 years. The Intergovernmental Panel on Climate Change (IPCC), which includes more than 1,300 scientists from the United States and other countries, forecasts a temperature rise of 2.5 to 10 degrees Fahrenheit over the next century. This warming will induce increased melting of the ice caps with significant sea level rise; the IPCC foresees a rise as high as three feet this century. A study led by former NASA climate scientist James Hansen (now at Columbia University) suggests sea level rise will be much higher—upward of ten feet—but this has not been peer-reviewed, and other scientists are skeptical. The ten feet Hansen predicts would make many of the world's coastal cities, such as New York and Miami, unlivable. Three feet would put many of New York's airport runways underwater, but this might be mitigated with seawalls. The other major effect of climate change is the potential for unprecedented weather events, with both extreme flooding and extreme droughts becoming more frequent. Food production likely will be affected in unprecedented ways, and this could cause massive migration of people not unlike the Syrian refugee crisis, only worse. Africa, with the world's fastest population growth, is particularly vulnerable to spreading drought, and in fact drought is occurring now in much of southern Africa and has put more than 50 million people at risk.

We must end the denial of climate change. As dire as the projections are for this century, warming is not going to stop there. By 2300, with unmitigated emissions assumptions, IPCC projects between three and ten feet of sea level rise. So, we must urgently use our creative scientific knowledge to figure out how to reduce the rapid increase in carbon dioxide and its warming effect on the planet and begin aggressive adaptation measures to meet inevitable climate change and sea level rise.

The planet also may be reaching its maximum carrying capacity of people. The Global Footprint Network (GFN) is an alliance of scientists that calculates how many Earths we would need to sustain our current growth rates. The GFN measures how much land and water area we need to produce the resources we consume and to absorb our waste, using prevailing technology. The GFN calculates that humanity is already exceeding the earth's sustainable productivity, so we are likely eating into our children's future. In his final book, *Brief Answers to the Big Questions*, Stephen Hawking said that at the present rate of population growth, by the year 2600 the world's population would literally be standing shoulder to shoulder! Clearly, this exponential population growth and consumption level cannot continue if we are to have a sustainable planet.

Humankind's "dominion" over the earth and all living things (as interpreted from the book of Genesis) is resulting in unprecedented environmental degradation that if not checked could have disastrous effects within the lifetime of my grandchildren. I read a truly scary book recently—*The God Species: Saving the Planet in the Age of Humans* by Mark Lynas, published by National Geographic. In it, the author reports on an expert group of twenty-nine leading scientists from around the world who have identified nine "planetary boundaries" that are increasingly of concern due to detrimental human activity, including climate change, biodiversity, pollution, land use, and ocean acidification. Uniquely in this century—within the lifetime of my grandchildren—we will likely reach the tipping point on several of these planetary environmental factors unless we soon take policy actions to slow the rate of deterioration of the planet and its species. So, it is profoundly sad to see so many of our political leaders in complete denial. In fact, there seems to be a race to consume all the fossil fuels, developed over millions of years on earth, within this century, and that race is one of the biggest contributors to greenhouse gas emissions and climate warming.

NASA recently reported that 2020 tied with 2016 as the hottest years on record. The past five years each rank among the five hottest since record-keeping began, and nineteen of the hottest twenty years have occurred during the past two decades. The disappearance of Arctic ice is one of the other most obvious indicators of global warming; its disappearance over the next several decades could eliminate an entire marine ecosystem. This illustrates one of the nine planetary boundaries: biodiversity. Lynas suggests in his book that a quarter of the world's mammals, a third of amphibians, and a quarter of warm-water coral are threatened with extinction. Our nearest relatives, the great apes, are among the most threatened mammals. In Africa, the gorillas in Virunga National Park in the Congo and northern Rwanda are increasingly threatened from poaching; their numbers are down to under four hundred. Margaret and I visited the park in northern Rwanda in 2011, and I have included a picture here of a gorilla mother and baby among a family of fourteen gorillas we observed. We were happy to hear that the governments are closely monitoring the gorilla families and providing more enforcement against poachers, yet the world's gorilla population remains at significant risk.

"Gorillas in the mist," Rwanda, 2011

Nitrogen pollution from increased use of fertilizer for agriculture is another threat. Although it is a great boon to our ability to produce enough food for the global population, we must find ways to make nitrogen use more efficient and environmentally compatible. Organic farming, although gaining popularity, cannot produce nearly the crop yields of land treated with nitrogen-based fertilizer. Producing the same yield from organic farming would require much more land cultivation. Genetic engineering (GE) is one of the ways to produce more nitrogen-efficient food crops. The US Food and Drug Administration assesses all GE foods to make sure they are safe before allowing them to be sold, but nevertheless, many consumer and environmental groups fight GE.

Other environmental concerns include land use, freshwater availability, aerosol pollution, ocean acidification, ozone depletion, and waste disposal, including the increasing problem of plastics. Unfortunately, extraordinarily little is being done politically on these issues. After successes such as the Montreal Protocol in 1988, aimed at a worldwide ban on CFCs to protect the ozone layer, politicians have been retreating from environmental issues.

Climate Change

The Trump administration in 2017 and 2018 released the government's Fourth National Climate Assessment (in two separate volumes), which is mandated by Congress.[57] The report, prepared by thirteen government agencies' top scientists and academic experts and peer-reviewed by the National Academy of Sciences, calls human activity the dominant driver of global warming. The report affirms that climate change is driven almost entirely by human action and warns of potential sea level rise by between one and four feet by the year 2100, noting that in the worst case, the rise could go as high as eight feet. The report highlights climate-related damage across the United States that is already happening because of an average global temperature increase of 1.8 degrees Fahrenheit since 1900, and it affirms that the US is already experiencing more extreme heat and rainfall events and more large wildfires in the West and that more than twenty-five coastal US cities are vulnerable to storm flooding. Houston, for example, has had multiple five-hundred-year storms in recent decades.

There is some good news as global energy-related CO2 emissions flattened in 2019 following two years of increases. This resulted mainly from a decline in CO2 emissions from the power sector in advanced economies. The NOAA reports that atmospheric carbon dioxide (CO_2) levels still remain high with the average for May 2019 peaking at nearly 415 ppm at NOAA's Mauna Loa Atmospheric Baseline Observatory in Hawaii (see accompanying figure showing CO_2 levels over the last 400,000 years). Monthly CO_2 values first passed the 400-ppm threshold in 2014, a level that had long been viewed as a limit we should not exceed if we expected to keep global average temperatures from rising more than two degrees Celsius (3.6 degrees Fahrenheit) by 2100—a level beyond which many scientists believe the planet will suffer irreversible impacts from extreme warming.

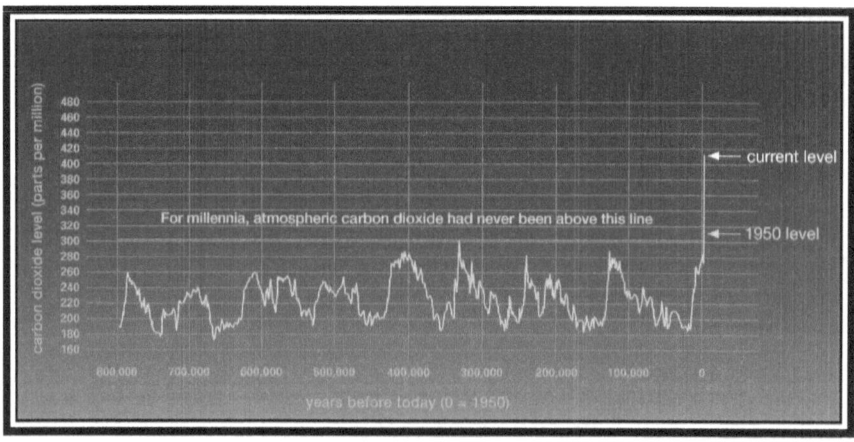

Carbon dioxide levels over last 400,000 years (source: NASA)

A new study from NASA and the European Space Agency, released in late 2019, reports that the Greenland ice sheet is melting more rapidly than previously thought.[58] The study published in *Nature* is the result of an international collaboration between eighty-nine polar scientists from fifty scientific institutions. They combined twenty-six independent satellite data sets to track global warming's effect on the Greenland ice sheet. Increasing rates of global warming have accelerated Greenland's ice mass loss from 25 billion tons per year in the 1990s to a current average of 234 billion tons per year. This means that Greenland's ice is melting on average seven times faster today than it was in the early 1990s, and thus global sea levels are also rising faster and are trending toward the most pessimistic scenarios for sea level rise earlier developed by climate scientists. The Greenland ice sheet holds enough water to raise the sea level by an astounding twenty-four feet. The international team previously reported in 2018 that ice losses from Antarctica have tripled since 2012, and it is a much larger threat for long-term sea level rise than Greenland.

Our planet also got a bad health report from the United Nations in May 2019. The assessment is contained in the sixth Global Environmental Outlook. The UN report highlights that although there have been positive efforts on a number of fronts, the planet's condition has continued to deteriorate since the first global outlook was prepared in 1997, and "urgent action at an unprecedented scale is necessary to arrest and reverse this situation." The report goes on to say that environmental policy efforts are being hindered by a variety of factors, in particular unsustainable human production and consumption patterns which have degraded the Earth's ecosystems, endangering the ecological foundations of society." The report concludes,

> Urgent action at an unprecedented scale is necessary to arrest and reverse this situation, thereby protecting human and environmental

health and maintaining the current and future integrity of global ecosystems. Key actions include reducing land degradation, biodiversity loss, and air, land, and water pollution; improving water management and resource management; climate change mitigation and adaptation; resource efficiency; addressing decarbonization, decoupling and detoxification; and the prevention and management of risk and disasters.[59]

The science community's conclusions are starkly at odds with an outgoing US administration that was in denial of US and world scientific findings about human-induced climate change and other environmental challenges and that actively rolled back environmental regulations intended to stem greenhouse gas emissions and other negative environmental consequences. Trump famously described climate change as a "hoax," and former EPA administrator Scott Pruitt said that he did not think human-produced carbon dioxide is driving climate change. Pruitt's agency scrubbed references to climate change from its website and barred its scientists from presenting scientific reports on the subject. Most embarrassingly and tragically, the Trump administration pulled the US out of the Paris international climate accord, leaving us standing alone as the only country in the world not signing the accord! This was terribly sad for a country that has the top scientists in the world and has been looked to as the leader in science and technology advances. Not only is our reputation diminished in the world's eyes, but this also sent a terrible signal to our young students who are considering careers in the science fields. With our national leaders so casually denying scientific facts and the findings of our best scientists, why would young students be attracted to a field commanding so little respect? National and state government leaders' denial of science also can affect our teachers and their ability or willingness to teach students about climate change honestly, accurately, and confidently.

Climate denial and its funding by fossil fuel and other interests clearly echo an earlier attempt to challenge scientific consensus—the campaign by the big tobacco companies to dispute the link between smoking and cancer. Although the tobacco companies knew as far back as the 1950s that the science was sound, they funded a body of widely disseminated research designed to throw doubt on that view. Their goal was to keep the public uncertain about the dangers of cigarettes and therefore to keep as many of them as possible, including young people, smoking for as long as possible. It was a dangerous and cynical business strategy, and in some cases, it was criminal as well. It worked to the extent that it bought the tobacco industry time to reorient its investment and marketing to take account of the new reality. But in the long run it failed. No reasonable person—and certainly no serious politician—now doubts the link between smoking and cancer. The fate of tobacco gives some hope that science can eventually win over climate skeptics.

Two scientific papers published by the journals *Science* and *Geophysical Research Letters* in 2014 came to similar conclusions about melting glaciers and ice sheets by different means. Both groups of scientists found that West Antarctic glaciers had retreated to a point that has set off an inherent instability in the ice sheet, something that experts have feared for decades. The melting of ice sheets in both Greenland and Antarctica will increasingly lead to sea level rise. The International Plant Protection Convention (IPPC) has warned that the global sea level could rise as much as three feet by the end of this century (and far worse in subsequent centuries) if stronger efforts are not made to control greenhouse gases. A recent Gallup poll on this topic shows that a majority of Americans believe that the effects of global warming are happening or will begin to happen during their lifetimes. At the same time, many fewer, currently about 36 percent, believe global warming will pose a serious threat to their way of life during their lifetimes. What about their children and grandchildren? My grandchildren most likely will be living by the end of the twenty-first century, when it is predicted that the effects of climate change already will have had dramatic effects on seal level rise, more severe weather patterns, and limits on food production due to a hotter and drier climate in key agricultural areas, among other severe impacts.

In no place in the United States is the sea level rise threat greater than in south Florida. Miami is exceptionally vulnerable because of its unique geology; the city is built on top of porous limestone, which is already allowing the rising seas to soak into the city's foundation. "Sea level rise is our reality in Miami Beach," according to the city's mayor, Philip Levine. "We are past the point of debating the existence of climate change and are now focusing on adapting to current and future threats." In the face of this serious threat, Florida's Senator Rubio (from south Florida) was quoted as saying, "I think all science deserves skepticism … Our climate is always changing. And what they have chosen to do is take a handful of decades of research and say that this is now evidence of a longer-term trend that's directly and almost solely attributable to man-made activities." But in response to a question, Senator Rubio was unable to provide the source(s) for his climate skepticism. This science skepticism is part of a disturbing trend that is particularly prevalent among conservative Republicans. Their orthodoxy and suspicion of government and science agencies has led to increasing denial regardless of mounting scientific evidence. For a country that has been a world leader in science and technology for so long, this is truly a sad trend. Not surprisingly, this climate denial effort has links to lobbying groups with self-interest in the fossil fuel industry. Greenpeace reports, for example, that the Koch brothers donated over $67 million to think tanks and organizations working on anti-climate agendas between 1997 and 2011. This is in contrast to other wealthy individuals and their foundations, such as Bill Gates and Warren Buffett, who donate a large chunk of their wealth to the common good in areas such as poverty, education, and health.

As the climate has warmed, sea levels have been rising about one to two millimeters per year due to the reduction in volume of ice caps, ice fields, and mountain glaciers, in addition to the thermal expansion of ocean water. If present trends continue, including an increase in global temperatures caused by increased greenhouse gas emissions, many of the world's mountain glaciers will disappear. Greenland's ice sheet loss is currently the single largest driver of sea level rise globally. But the real threat is in Antarctica, which has about 90 percent of the earth's polar ice sheet, and as mentioned earlier, the Antarctic Peninsula reached a record temperature in February 2020.

Image of receding Greenland glacier (NASA)

Pope Francis issued an important encyclical on the environment in 2015 titled *On Care for Our Common Home*, calling on us all to be good stewards of God's creation. The pope, who studied chemistry and worked as a chemist before entering the seminary, has a history of environmental concern. The pope contends that science is largely settled on the causes of climate change and that greater stewardship of God's creation is necessary. Pope Francis goes on to say this in his encyclical letter:

> A very solid scientific consensus indicates that we are presently witnessing a disturbing warming of the climatic system. In recent decades, this warming has been accompanied by a constant rise in the sea level and, it would appear, by an increase of extreme weather events, even

if a scientifically determinable cause cannot be assigned to each particular phenomenon. Humanity is called to recognize the need for changes of lifestyle, production, and consumption, in order to combat this warming or at least the human causes which produce or aggravate it ... If present trends continue, this century may well witness extraordinary climate change and an unprecedented destruction of ecosystems, with serious consequences for all of us ...

The pope further said,

This sister now cries out to us because of the harm we have inflicted on her by our irresponsible use and abuse of the goods with which God has endowed her. We have come to see ourselves as her lords and masters, entitled to plunder her at will. The violence present in our hearts, wounded by sin, is also reflected in the symptoms of sickness evident in the soil, in the water, in the air and in all forms of life. This is why the earth herself, burdened and laid waste, is among the most abandoned and maltreated of our poor; she "groans in travail" (Rom 8:22). We have forgotten that we ourselves are dust of the earth (cf. Gen 2:7); our very bodies are made up of her elements, we breathe her air, and we receive life and refreshment from her waters.

As the pope writes, humans must make changes in lifestyle and consumption "in order to combat this warming or at least the human causes which produce or aggravate it." It is true that there are other factors (e.g., volcanic activity, variations in the earth's orbit and axis, the solar cycle), yet a number of scientific studies indicate that most global warming in recent decades is due to the great concentration of greenhouse gases (carbon dioxide, methane, nitrogen oxides, and others) released mainly as a result of human activity. As these gases build up in the atmosphere, they hamper the escape of heat produced by sunlight at the earth's surface. The problem is aggravated by a model of development based on the intensive use of fossil fuels, which is at the heart of the worldwide energy system.

Mass Extinction

Since the origin of life on earth some 3.8 billion years ago, our planet has experienced five mass extinction events. The last of these events occurred some 66 million years ago, when a six-mile-wide asteroid is thought to have collided with Earth, wiping out the dinosaurs. The Cretaceous extinction event dramatically changed the composition of biodiversity on the planet; marine ecosystems essentially collapsed, and about 75 percent of all plant and animal species disappeared. Today, according to Elizabeth Kolbert, author of the book *Sixth Extinction*, we are witnessing a similar mass extinction event right before our eyes. This time, however, a giant asteroid is not to blame—it is humans who are altering environmental conditions on the planet so swiftly and dramatically that a large proportion of other species cannot adapt. According to E. O. Wilson, the present extinction rate in the tropics is "on the order of 10,000 times greater than the naturally occurring background extinction rate" and will reduce biological diversity to its lowest level since the last great extinction. If we are to stem this extinction rate, we will have to focus on restoring habitats, controlling alien species, reducing pollution of estuaries, preserving rainforests, and addressing climate change, among other measures. We have a moral obligation to protect our planet and its many amazing species, including humans, from mass extinction.

Current National and International Environmental Efforts

In the last fifty-plus years, three Republican presidents signed into law sweeping environmental laws that have dramatically improved our nation's air quality, cleaned our waters, and protected the ozone layer. These presidents embraced scientific findings of the time showing the significant threat to public health and the physical environment. The hugely successful Clean Air Act was signed by President Richard Nixon on December 31, 1970, to foster improved human health and protect the environment. President Nixon said in signing the bill, "I think that 1970 will be known as the year of the beginning, in which we really began to move on the problems of clean air and clean water and open spaces for the future generations of America," and he was proven right as we look back nearly fifty years later. President Reagan followed in the 1980s with the signing of the Montreal Protocol, an international environmental treaty that helped save the ozone layer in the upper atmosphere, which protects the planet and its people from debilitating levels of cancer-causing ultraviolet radiation. The gases that were destroying the ozone layer (e.g., chlorofluorocarbons, or CFCs) also happen to be powerful greenhouse gases, so their elimination under the treaty also helped stem climate warming. The Montreal Protocol negotiated by the Reagan administration is widely seen as the most successful global environmental treaty. The treaty was negotiated under the United Nations Environment Program and required at least eleven of the major emitting countries to sign by January 1989 to go into effect. Amazingly, the US led the way, with the Senate unanimously approving the treaty. Can you imagine that kind of bipartisan support today for an international environmental treaty?

The Montreal treaty was followed relatively shortly by extremely important domestic environmental legislation, when George H. W. Bush signed the extension of the Clean Air Act (S1630). He said on signing the milestone bill in 1990, "I take great pleasure in signing S. 1630 as a demonstration to the American people of my determination that each and every American shall breathe clean air." The 1990 amendments required even lower motor vehicle tailpipe emissions and more stringent emission-testing procedures that, building on the 1970 act, have resulted in dramatic improvements in our nation's air quality. The EPA reported in 2020 that since 1990, there has been a nearly 60 percent reduction in mercury from human sources such as coal-fired plants, a 66 percent decline in benzene, and an 84 percent fall in lead, which harms brain development in children. Further, the 1990 Clean Air Act for the first time included a market-based cap-and-trade approach to drastically cut sulfur emissions (acid rain) from power plants, which were harming forests and waterways; this provision was more successful and less costly than forecast at the time. The rapid global decline in ozone-depleting substances also shows that we can make positive change when we act decisively.

Yet today, when we are facing perhaps the greatest environmental threat to the planet and its inhabitants—that is, climate change—there is no bipartisan consensus or leadership.

The party of Nixon, Reagan, and George H. W. Bush, which led the bipartisan milestone environmental accomplishments of the last four decades, has turned to strong resistance or outright denial of climate science, particularly among party hardliners. One of the problems seems to be that many politicians and American voters do not view climate change, as compared to environmental issues of the past, as an immediate threat. Yet the IPPC has warned that without global action, climate change will increase the likelihood of severe, pervasive, and irreversible impacts for people and ecosystems. Echoing that dire warning, UN Secretary-General Ban Ki-Moon said that if the world maintains its "business as usual" attitude about climate change, the opportunity to keep temperature rise below the international target of two degrees Celsius "will slip away within the next decade."

The National Academy of Sciences finds that climate change from increased greenhouse gas concentration poses significant risks to human society and the environment. Yet many on the political and religious right deny climate change entirely and/ or that it has any human cause and have helped stall efforts to address the issue. At the same time, they claim to be for protection of family values. To me this is a contradiction because protecting the planet for our children and grandchildren is very much pro-family. Progressives and conservatives should be able to seek common agreement to preserve this marvelous creation and to pass it relatively unspoiled to our grandchildren, so that they will have a healthy, inhabitable planet for themselves and the amazing variety of earth's species, which are increasingly threatened.

The lack of any action in Congress on these serious climate issues led President Obama to pursue climate initiatives primarily through regulatory approaches, for which the Supreme

Court found he had the authority. In order to achieve a goal of economy-wide greenhouse house gas emission reductions by 2020 in the range of 17 percent below 2005 levels, the Obama administration adopted the toughest fuel economy and greenhouse gas emission standards for passenger vehicles in US history, requiring an average performance equivalent of 54.5 miles per gallon. Further, the Obama administration tightened the carbon pollution standards for both new and existing power plants. Shifting from coal- to gas-fired power plants is the main reason US greenhouse gas emissions fell for much of the last decade, up until 2018, when emissions again increased.

Unfortunately, the Trump administration rolled back many Obama-era climate regulations and policies. For example, under the Trump administration's revised automobile fuel and emissions standards, fuel efficiency would increase only 1.5 percent each year through model year 2026, as compared with the standards issued in 2012, which would have required about 5 percent annual increases. Unfortunately, the nation was for four years in the hands of a president and party that dismissed actions to slow climate change in favor of fossil fuel development. President Trump made it official early in his administration that the United States would withdraw from the Paris climate accord, although there was a four-year withdrawal process which recently went into effect. We were in the situation under Trump of sitting on the sidelines as the other 197 countries in the world worked together under the provisions of the climate agreement. The Paris climate accord follow-up in Bonn, Germany, in late 2017 was revealing—many US governors and businesses actively participated while administration representatives sat on the sidelines! Many in America's corporate leadership support the Paris climate accord. They recognized that we must be in the game to influence the outcome, and they understand that coal is never coming back as the dominant energy source and that even oil's future is eventually limited. Further, we ceded the renewable energy future to China, which is heavily investing in solar. Despite the United States' withdrawal, the other countries of the world moved ahead with the Paris climate accord. In late 2018 in Poland, countries thrashed out the complex details of how to account for and record their greenhouse gas emissions as they put the Paris Agreement goals into action. But difficult questions such as how to scale up existing commitments on cutting emissions and how to provide finance for poor countries to do the same were put off for future years. The United States was booed at the meeting as it advocated for fossil fuel development, including more coal! Fortunately, the new Biden administration just rejoined the Paris climate agreement, so that is good news for America and the world. We must all be part of the global struggle to confront this most formidable challenge to the planet and its inhabitants.

Global carbon emissions reached an all-time high in 2019 as CO2 emissions from fossil fuel combustion rose by an estimated 0.6 percent. Fossil fuel emissions in the US have fallen significantly since 2005, in significant part because of a boom in cheaper and plentiful natural gas and, to a lesser extent, in renewable energy, which have been rapidly displacing dirtier coal-fired power. But that conversion slowed, particularly with the Trump administration's push for more coal use; further exacerbating the effort to reduce climate emissions was the Trump administration's rollback of vehicle emission and fuel standards.

Fossil fuels in the earth are hundreds of millions of years old, but we are intent on depleting them in a matter of two hundred years, leaving no fossil fuel reserves for future generations but rather leaving them rapid climate change that will be detrimental for our children and grandchildren. How selfish of us, yet we want to extract every drop, even in our national parks. There are currently more than five hundred active oil and gas wells spread across twelve national parks. In 2015, drilling on federal lands made up nearly a fifth of overall US production.

The current food system is a major driver of climate change, particularly the production of animal products, which generates the majority of food-related greenhouse gas emissions and other environmental degradation. Today, only a bit over half of the world's crop calories feed people directly; the rest are mostly fed to livestock. Eating less meat and dairy and more plant-based foods will be vital to reducing our carbon footprint and other environmental degradation.

Much of the planet sweltered in unprecedented heat in the summer of 2019. In July, temperatures soared to new heights in the hottest month ever recorded. The record warmth shrank Arctic and Antarctic sea ice to historic lows. The average global temperature in July was 1.71 degrees Fahrenheit above the twentieth-century average, making it the hottest July in the 140-year record, according to scientists at the NOAA's National Centers for Environmental Information. Nine of the ten hottest Julys have occurred since 2005—with the last five years ranking as the five hottest. July 2019 was also the forty-third consecutive July and 415th consecutive month with above-average global temperatures.

In a related development, 2019 and 2020 brought a dramatic increase in wildfires in some Arctic regions that traditionally have rarely burned. Since July 2019, fire has charred about six million acres of Siberian forest, an area roughly the size of the state of Vermont. In Alaska, fires have consumed more than 2.5 million acres of tundra and snow forest, leading researchers to suggest that the combination of climate change and wildfires could permanently alter the region's forests. And we had the tragic mass burning in the Amazon. The Amazon rainforest produces about 20 percent of the world's oxygen and is often called "the planet's lungs." According to the World Wildlife Fund, if it is irrevocably damaged, the Amazon could start emitting carbon instead, leading to even more warming of the planet.

The government's 2018 National Climate Assessment concluded that the warming caused by greenhouse gases has already led to worsening wildfires and crop failures and could affect the future American economy. In the face of these disturbing climate findings, the Trump administration continued to try to roll back environmental/climate regulations to favor industry, particularly fossil fuel industries, while jeopardizing the sustainability of our planet and future populations. The Trump EPA in mid-2020 proposed a far-reaching plan to cut back on the regulation of methane emissions, a major contributor to climate change. The EPA's proposed rule aimed to eliminate federal requirements that oil and gas companies install technology to detect and fix methane leaks from wells, pipelines, and storage facilities. It also reopened the question of whether the EPA has the legal authority to regulate methane as a pollutant.

As mentioned previously, the Trump administration issued regulations to roll back auto efficiency standards. The new regulations require fuel economy averages for passenger cars at 43.7 mpg, down from the 54.5 mpg standard set for 2025 during the Obama administration. For all vehicles, the average would be 37.0 mpg, down from the 46.7 mpg Obama standard. Trump sought to open millions of acres of public land and water to drilling, including the Arctic National Wildlife Refuge, and has lifted an Obama-era moratorium on new coal mining leases on public land. The Interior Department completed a plan to weaken the Endangered Species Act, and the EPA weakened clean-water regulations affecting streams and wetlands. Most of these rollbacks by the Trump Administration will be reversed by the new Biden Administration. And on the day of Biden's Inauguration, he brought the country back into the Paris Climate Accord!

Recently, there was more disturbing environmental news as Australian authorities sounded the alarm about the health of the Great Barrier Reef's coral. The habitat was already in bad condition, but now the status has been officially downgraded from "poor" to "very poor." The Australian government said in its *Great Barrier Reef Outlook Report* released in 2019, "The significant and large-scale impacts from record-breaking sea surface temperatures have resulted in coral reef habitat transitioning from poor to very poor condition." We visited the Great Barrier Reef some years ago, and it was a remarkable experience to see the expansive coral reef and the multiplicity of sea life swimming among the coral. Now my grandchildren could well be deprived of ever seeing this world treasure. And of course, coral reefs around the world are being threatened because of rising sea temperatures, resulting from the absorption of increased levels of carbon dioxide in the atmosphere; the sea absorbs about half of the increased carbon levels. In early 2020, Australia was reeling from massive fires throughout large sections of the continent that are almost certainly climate related. Yet politicians in Australia continue to deny much of the climate science and call for more fossil fuel development. It is so sad to see a whole continent at risk and little political leadership to confront the challenge.

Because of global environmental concerns, Secretary-General of the United Nations António Guterres held a special session of the UN on September 21, 2019, in New York. Guterres said at the time,

> Despite years of talk, global emissions are reaching record levels and show no sign of peaking. The concentration of carbon dioxide in our atmosphere is the highest it has been in 3 million years. The last four years were the four hottest on record, and winter temperatures in the Arctic have risen by 3–4°C in the last 50 years. Sea levels are rising, coral reefs are dying, and we are starting to see the life-threatening impact of climate change on health, through air pollution, heatwaves, and risks to food security … That is why I am bringing world leaders together at a climate action summit later this year.

In the face of this mounting global concern, the US was sitting on the sidelines; in fact, it was proposing actions to make the climate challenge worse.

In their new book *The Future We Choose: Surviving the Climate Crisis*, Christiana Figueres and Tom Rivett-Carnac, two of the lead negotiators of the Paris climate agreement, lay out the urgency of our climate decisions. They say that in the coming decade, we are facing an enormously consequential fork in the road. If we continue as now, we will be going irreparably down a course of destruction, with much human pain and biodiversity loss. Or we can choose to go in the other direction, on a path that at least diminishes the negative impacts of climate change to something manageable. The authors posit that it is already too late to solve the climate crisis. They make the case that consumption is at the core of what is happening to our planet. This challenges our basic assumptions about continuing economic growth supported largely by consumerism. We must all make lifestyle changes toward a green economy that results in a much more sustainable energy and environmental path forward. The authors say that "the goal of halving global emissions by 2030 is the absolute minimum we must achieve if we are to have at least a 50 percent chance of safeguarding humanity from the worst impacts."

Politically, this is becoming a more important issue every year. As of mid-2019, 84 percent of Democrats and Democratic-leaning independents said climate change is a major threat to the country's well-being, up from 58 percent in March 2013, according to a Pew Research Center survey. That compares with 27 percent of Republicans and Republican-leaning independents, up from 22 percent in 2013. The growing concern has spurred a relatively new grassroots environmental advocacy group, the Environmental Voter Project, which strived to engage five million new voters in 2020. Young people worldwide are engaged on the climate issue, and many attended the UN summit in New York, led by sixteen-year-old Greta Thunberg of Sweden, who has gained a worldwide following.

Solutions will not be easy, but they are possible. In the US, there is no solid bipartisan approach evident today, although each chamber of Congress has established a bipartisan Climate Solutions Caucus in recent years as a forum for discussing options among their members. At the same time, a relatively new bipartisan Climate Leadership Council, including energy companies and environmental groups, has proposed a plan for an economy-wide fee on CO_2 emissions starting at $40 a ton (in 2017 dollars), with rebates to all citizens in an attempt to make the plan revenue-neutral.[60] The goal of the plan is to cut emissions in half by 2035. In an encouraging letter sent to Congress and the Biden transition team in late 2020, more than forty major US companies say they support rejoining the Paris climate accord, and urge "President-elect Biden and the new Congress to work together to enact ambitious, durable, bipartisan climate solutions." The new Biden administration's climate goal is to have the United States achieve a 100 percent clean energy economy and reach net-zero emissions no later than 2050. Hopefully, future generations can look back at this time as a key global turning point for the planet. The climate effort will be just as challenging as issues faced by our parents and grandparents in the world wars and the Great Depression, when they sacrificed so that we would have a better life. Our children and grandchildren will be the beneficiaries or the victims of our decisions.

8

The Global Common Good

The concept of the common good compels us to increasingly recognize our global citizenship and concern for all humanity and the environmental sustainability of the planet we share. Areas such as universal human rights, climate change, economic justice, peace initiatives, support for refugees, and the like are of increasing concern. Many organizations, such as Human Rights Watch, Save the Children, Amnesty International, Mercy Corps International, Refugees International, and others, focus attention on these global issues.

Too much of the world's resources goes toward warfare. President Eisenhower, who was decorated as our Allied commander in World War II, had these words inscribed above his tomb:

Inscription on President Eisenhower's tomb

"Every gun made, every warship launched, every rocket fired signifies, in the final sense, a theft from those who hunger and are not fed, those who are cold and are not clothed . . . This is not a way of life at all . . . . Under the cloud of threatening war, it is humanity hanging from a cross of iron."

"The Chance for Peace" Address, Washington, D.C.
April 16, 1953

Global poverty and economic development—As recently as the 1960s, a majority of humans lived in extreme poverty. Now fewer than 10 percent live in extreme poverty according to Max Roser, an Oxford University economist, who runs the website Our World in Data. With the onset of industrialization and rising productivity, the share of people in extreme poverty has decreased continuously over the last two centuries. In recent decades, China's rise from poverty has made a particularly notable impact on world poverty; China reduced its extreme-poverty rate from 84 percent in 1980 to about 10 percent now. This dramatic global reduction in poverty is a remarkable achievement of humankind, though much remains to be done. According to the UN Sustainable Development Goals report of 2019, extreme poverty has declined considerably, the under-five mortality rate fell by 49 percent between 2000 and 2017, immunizations have saved millions of lives, and the vast majority of the world's population now has access to electricity.[61] But the report also notes that global hunger is on the rise, at least half of the world's population lacks essential health services, and women in most parts of the world continue to face structural disadvantages and discrimination, among other findings.

Health care—The matter of health care is of vital concern globally. Every year around 10 million people in poorer countries die of illnesses that could be very cheaply prevented or managed, including malaria, HIV, tuberculosis, and diarrhea. Progress is being made, and there are notable examples of improvements in developing countries' healthcare systems and outcomes. We have personally witnessed the development of a near universal healthcare system in Rwanda during its remarkable social and economic recovery from the 1994 genocide. Medical authorities report that more than 97 percent of Rwandan infants are vaccinated in accord with international health protocols.

Global refugees and immigration issues—The UN Refugee Agency reports that by the end of 2018, 70.8 million individuals were forcibly displaced worldwide as a result of persecution, conflict, violence, or human rights violations. That was an increase of 2.3 million people over the previous year. This includes.

- 25.9 million refugees—the highest ever seen;
- 41.3 million internally displaced people; and
- 3.5 million asylum-seekers.

Syria continues to be the largest source of refugees. According to the UN, 12 million Syrians—more than half the country's population—have been forced from their homes. Education is often a casualty for children caught up in conflict and persecution. Today, less than a quarter of the world's nearly two million secondary school–aged refugee adolescents attend school. Girls are often most affected. At the same time that the world is seeing an unusually high number of refugees, governments, including in the US, are building walls, or otherwise denying entrance to refugees who have no home. Unfortunately, as the climate changes, there are likely to be more refugees due to drought, sea level rise, catastrophic weather events, and the like.

Equality of women—Globally, women have fewer opportunities for economic participation than men, less access to education, greater health and safety risks, and less political representation. Guaranteeing the rights of women and giving them equal opportunities is a critical challenge. Empowered women and girls contribute to the health and productivity of their families, communities, and countries, thus benefiting everyone. Globally, the proportion of women aged twenty to twenty-four who report that they were married before their eighteenth birthdays has dropped, but the figure still stood at 26 percent in 2015. In thirty countries where the practice of female genital mutilation is concentrated, more than a third of girls aged fifteen to nineteen have undergone the procedure. Speaking ahead of the annual meeting of the UN Commission on the Status of Women in New York in March 2020, UN Secretary-General Guterres warned that the state of women's rights globally is dire, saying, "Just as slavery and colonialism were a stain on previous centuries, women's inequality should shame us all in the 21st. Because it is not only unacceptable; it is stupid … There is a strong and relentless pushback against women's rights … Women's sexual and reproductive rights are under threat from different sides." He further said that legal protections against rape and domestic violence are being diluted or rolled back and that in thirty-four countries rape within marriage is still legal.

Global sustainability—The most global of issues is sustainability of the planet. In the past two hundred years, the global population has increased from less than a billion to over seven billion today, and such a growth rate is unsustainable. This growth was made possible by exploitation of our natural resources, particularly fossil fuels, whose rapid consumption propelled our global economy but has greatly increased carbon dioxide concentrations in the atmosphere. Our rates of population growth, resource consumption, greenhouse gas emissions, waste products, and species degradation must be curbed in coming decades if we are to have a habitable planet by the end of the century and beyond. Actions in coming decades will help determine the sustainability of our planet for centuries to come. Pope Francis importantly says about climate change, "The climate is a common good, belonging to all and meant for all. At the global level, it is a complex system linked to many of the essential conditions for human life."

World conflict and peace seeking—The United Nations reports that in the past 15 years, more than half of the world's population has lived in proximity to significant political violence. Pew Research Center reports more than 20 million people have been displaced in the Middle East due to recent conflicts principally in Syria, Iraq, and Yemen. But the world is nowhere near as genocidal as it was during the 1940s, when Nazi, Soviet, and Japanese mass murders, together with the targeting of civilians by all sides in World War II, resulted in a civilian death rate in the vicinity of 350 per 100,000 per year. Stalin and Mao kept the global rate between 75 and 150 through the early 1960s, and it has been falling ever since. Steven Pinker says in his conclusion to his 2011 book *The Better Angels of Our Nature: Why Violence Has Declined*, "To review the history of violence is to be repeatedly astounded by the cruelty and waste of it all, and at times to be overcome with anger, disgust, and immeasurable sadness." But he then writes that "the decline of violence is an accomplishment we can savor, and an impetus to cherish the forces of civilization and enlightenment that made it possible."

On the other hand, we are seeing democratic erosion around the world. *Freedom in the World 2020*, the latest survey from Freedom House, shows that 2019 was the fourteenth year in a row of deterioration in political freedom, with sixty-four countries showing a loss of freedom and only thirty-seven experiencing improvements. Disturbingly, the US is among those showing deterioration in such areas as refugee treatment, media intimidation, and political interference in our court system. In her new book, *Twilight of Democracy, The Seductive Lure of Authoritarianism*, Anne Applebaum investigates the struggle between democracy and dictatorship with a focus on Poland and other countries of Eastern Europe where there seems to be a trend back toward authoritarianism. She suggests that authoritarianism appeals to people who do not like complexity and who are suspicious of people with different ideas. The good news in the Freedom House report is that more protest movements have emerged worldwide to press for freedom and justice.

Although we do not have the global wars of the twentieth century, we are engaged in multiple long-term conflicts, particularly in the Middle East. The Afghan war is approaching twenty years, and yet the fighting has continued without a clear purpose or exit strategy across three presidential administrations. Recently, there have been peace discussions with the Taliban, but results are uncertain. The war in Iraq, which started in 2003, continued in more recent years with the emergence of ISIS and spread over the border into Syria. Although ISIS has been mostly defeated in both countries, unrest is still at a high level. Almost two decades after the Bush White House projected American troops as liberators who would be welcomed with open arms, Iraq is still in extremely fragile condition, and the war spread to Syria via ISIS, which had its origins in Iraq. The US has at various times declared success along the way, but still the wars grind on, with the conflict in Afghanistan now receiving American soldiers born after it began! More than three million brave Americans have served in uniform in these wars, half of them in multiple tours of duty; all Americans owe this cadre of professional soldiers a debt of gratitude. For the rest of us, life goes on with little thought of the challenges they face daily. Tragically, nearly 7,000 of them have died. Tens of thousands more have been wounded. Millions of civilians have been killed or displaced in the Middle East as a result of these forever wars. The governments of Afghanistan and Iraq, each of which the United States spent hundreds of billions to build and support, are fragile at best.

Sadly, the United States' military involvement in the post-9/11 wars of the Middle East has cost trillions of dollars that could have done so much good here at home. Based on the Brown University comprehensive report "Costs of War," issued in 2011 and updated since, the US has spent or been obligated to spend over $6.4 trillion on the post-9/11 wars.[62] This spending has largely been financed by borrowing, so future interest on that debt will costs billions more. Further, more than 801,000 people have died due to direct war violence, and several times as many have been killed indirectly. More than 335,000 civilians have been killed as a result of the fighting, and there are an estimated 21 million war refugees and displaced persons.

The report further estimates that over 370,000 people—including US soldiers, contractors, allied security forces, and civilian bystanders—have died due to direct war violence in Iraq, Afghanistan, and Pakistan, and at least 200,000 civilians have been killed indirectly as a result of the fighting. The study estimates that war refugees and displaced persons now number over 10 million, including those affected by the war in Syria. The report also highlights the long-term trauma effects of war on our soldiers and their families. As mentioned earlier, over three million service members have been to the war zones of Iraq and Afghanistan since 2001, and over half have deployed multiple times. Many Iraq and Afghanistan veterans face a life of disability due to the physical and psychological injuries they sustained in the war zones. At least 970,000 veterans have some degree of officially recognized disability because of the wars. Many more live with physical and emotional scars but lack disability status. And the costs of war extend to families, who cope with their loved ones' absence, mourn their deaths, or deal with the changed person who often returns. The Veterans Administration only began tracking war veteran suicides in 2008, but data now show significantly higher rates among war veterans than among comparable civilians, and a 2010 report found that child abuse in army families has been three times higher in homes from which a parent was deployed. These tragic effects are unaccounted and/or unquantified in most studies of the wars' impacts.

These Middle East conflicts were happening when the US domestically was going through the Great Recession. Massive domestic economic dislocation and turmoil resulted that could have greatly benefited from even a portion of the trillions spent on these foreign wars. Yet the war spending goes on, and we see larger military budgets each year. The US military budget is greater than those of the next ten largest countries combined. This only exacerbates America's debt problem. The annual federal deficit is now well over $1 trillion and will continue to rise in the decade, and that was compounded by the need for massive stimulus to counter the effects of the coronavirus outbreak.

Christians developed the "just war theory" in the thirteenth century, but it has gradually evolved into a more universal theory of justification for war. Although Saint Augustine commented on the morality of war from the Christian perspective, the most systematic statement was developed by Saint Thomas Aquinas in the thirteenth century. In the *Summa Theologicae*, Aquinas presented the general outline of what would become the traditional just war theory. Aquinas's thoughts became the model for later scholars and legalists to expand on and gradually universalize beyond Christendom. The principles of justification for war are commonly held to be having just cause, being a last resort, being declared by a proper authority, possessing right intention, having a reasonable chance of success, and the end being proportional to the means used.[63] But all too often, the faithful are helping to lead the rush to war.

Unfortunately, during my lifetime, we have had at least two wars supported by many in the religious community that almost certainly did not meet the test of the just war theory: the Vietnam War and Second Gulf War (Iraq). In neither case was war justified as a last resort. Both saw presidents lying and abusing power to justify war expansion, one a Democrat, Lyndon Johnson, and the other a Republican, George W. Bush. In 2017, the ten-part PBS series on Vietnam by Ken Burns caused many to soul-search a bit more on lessons learned from a failed war. More than forty years after it ended, we are still reflecting on the Vietnam War, and we are still arguing about why it went wrong, who was to blame, and whether it was all worth it. As mentioned earlier, the US federal government has spent upward of $6 trillion on the post-9/11 wars in the Middle East, and this spending has been financed largely by borrowing, meaning future interest on that debt will costs billions more. Commentator Fareed Zakaria warns that it is easy to start a war, but it is exceedingly difficult to predict how it will go and where it might end. He suggests we need to ask some hard questions before we start launching missiles particularly in an era when unstable regimes now possess nuclear weapons.

We all need to be much more active and vocal in challenging the rush to war before other options are exhausted, as should have happened in the rush to war in Iraq with trumped-up claims of weapons of mass destruction at the highest levels of our government. Our nation must also use our soft power (e.g., diplomacy, sanctions) much more effectively before considering the use of hard power such as military action. As Joseph Nye suggests in his book *Soft Power*, "America's success will depend upon our developing a deeper understanding of the role of soft power and developing a better balance of hard and soft power in our foreign policy."[64] He calls that balanced approach "smart power."

For a positive view of what might be possible globally to advance humankind and the environment, one might look at the United Nations' visionary 2015 document for our global community titled *Transforming Our World: The 2030 Agenda for Sustainable Development*, which identifies seventeen sustainable development goals, including addressing poverty while stemming excess consumption and degradation of our planet, loss of species, and climate change. It offers a bold blueprint for an improved global society and sustainable planet.[65]

9

Achieving the Common Good through Public Policy

Following is a brief discussion of the public policy formulation process, followed by highlights of some of the more immediate common-good public policies I believe we need to tackle as a nation. Hopefully, we heed the words of Jefferson articulated nearly two and a half centuries ago, "The care of human life and happiness, and not their destruction, is the first and only legitimate object of government." I also provide perspectives on the role of advocacy and community organizing to help achieve these policies.

Changing Public Policy

Public policy formulation is too often a haphazard process with lots of detours along the way. For example, the effort to provide universal healthcare in this country continues to be one of the most tortuous public policy efforts in our nation's history, stretching over many decades. President Harry Truman called for universal healthcare as part of his Fair Deal in 1949, but strong opposition stopped it; however, in 1946 the National Mental Health Act, which had been one part of Truman's healthcare proposal, was passed. Substantial progress was made under President Johnson, with passage of Medicare and Medicaid in 1965. During the early 1970s, several universal health care bills were introduced in Congress, but none got enough support for enactment. In 1993, the Clinton-proposed healthcare plan included mandatory enrollment in a health insurance plan, subsidies to guarantee affordability across all income ranges, and the establishment of health alliances in each state, but it also ran into strong opposition. Finally, under President Obama, the ACA was passed in 2010, but the debate continues, with conservatives still trying to repeal or cut back the program. Additionally, just under 30 million Americans still are without coverage, so more is needed. There are various emerging proposals for universal health care through mechanisms such as expanding the ACA to include a public option or going to Medicare for All; these proposals were all on the Democratic side in the Presidential campaign of 2020. The winning democratic candidate and now President Joe Biden strongly prefers to build on the ACA with a public option. Now, given the COVID-19 crisis, it would be inexcusable not to move to universal health coverage.

One complicating public policy factor at this time is the tendency toward minority rule. Although the country has an emerging multiethnic majority, translating it into a governing majority has been difficult. The party with the most votes does not necessarily win in recent Presidential elections. Constitutional design and recent political and geographic trends have unfortunately emerged to produce what is effectively becoming minority rule. Our Constitution was designed to favor small states. Small states were given representation equal to that of big states in the Senate and an advantage in the Electoral College. What began as a minor advantage evolved, over time, has grown into a large advantage for small rural states. This overrepresentation of small rural states has resulted in a Republican advantaged Senate that has most recently stacked a conservative Supreme Court that increasingly does not represent our diverse America. And the electoral college advantage has resulted in recent Republican Presidents Bush and Trump becoming President without winning the popular vote. The Trump presidency, with a rural state advantaged Senate, has packed the courts at all levels with conservative judges often not representative of an emerging diverse America.

Political activism, including the large representation of women and minorities in recent elections, is helping change the face of our electorate and our representatives. The old boy networks are being challenged and this is a positive trend. In any case, to be effective in advancing any public policy issue seeking resolution, there are certain basic, key steps to implementation. For example, there should be a well-documented case for addressing the problem, clear objectives for change, identification of alternative pathways, specific program or policy solutions, sound funding proposals, bipartisan approaches, broad public engagement during the process, and formulation of well-thought-out legislative or other public policy paths to implementation for change. None of this guarantees success, but without these preparatory steps, chances of implementation are diminished.

Economic and Social Justice Policies

Economic opportunity is fundamental to a healthy progressive nation; unfortunately, as highlighted earlier, our nation is one of the most economically unequal nations in the developed world. Advocates of inclusive capitalism discussed earlier, say that the left and the right must be more flexible in addressing our nation's economic problems. They suggest that although some in both political parties seek to turn away from globalization and technological advancement, that is not a realistic option for our nation as we compete in an increasingly worldwide market. Businesses that do not adapt to new technology inevitably lose out in global competition. Inclusive-capitalism advocates embrace the need for successful entrepreneurs and wealth creation to finance new investment to achieve economic progress, but at the same time they emphasize that labor must benefit as well if we are to have a successful economy. They further suggest that those on the right who argue for a return to laissez-faire, trickle-down economics, which includes cutting taxes at the top, eliminating regulation, and making deep cuts to safety-net programs, are misguided because this will only lead to a nation that is more and more unequal. The advocates of inclusive capitalism wish to create a more inclusive economy with good jobs, decent salaries, and a hopeful future for all its citizens. They see this as possible but acknowledge that it will require a concerted effort and a major shift in policy across several areas. They say that powerful forces of globalization and technological change must be navigated, or inequalities will continue to widen, and for many, low-skill work will increasingly become the norm. We need political leadership that embraces the core principles that truly make America great; those principles embrace freedom and equality and include an appreciation of the intrinsic worth of every human being, no matter their race, ethnic origin, or religion.

We must remember, however, that every important progressive policy success in American history that facilitated the common good, including abolition, women's suffrage, labor rights, a progressive income tax, Social Security, civil rights, Medicare, and marriage equality, has required compromises in persuading potential allies who may have different political or policy views. Purity in one's political position, although seemingly virtuous, seldom leads to fundamental change in society. Proposals such as free college education for all, free health care for all, free childcare and early education, and the like sound appealing but will not likely command majorities in the legislative bodies; our democratic system will always require some compromises.

Based on the key social, economic, and environmental challenges discussed in earlier chapters, here are some key policy responses that I believe warrant national consideration.

Some key policies to address economic challenges

- **Move toward a living wage or universal basic income**—Too many people working full-time jobs (or even two or three of them) do not make enough to get by in normal times, let alone a crisis like COVID-19. A study by the National Employment Law Project found that $15/hour was the lowest wage that would still allow a single worker to meet the basic cost of living just about everywhere in the United States.[66] There are a variety of ways to assure a living wage, including minimum-wage legislation, the Earned Income Tax Credit discussed elsewhere, and wage enhancement. Former Democratic presidential candidate Andrew Yang called for a monthly basic income that would be provided permanently to American adults. Now that a temporary income support has been provided to low- and moderate-income families during the coronavirus crisis, maybe we should reconsider this idea for the longer term.

- **Guarantee paid sick and family leave**—Workplace benefits are an important part of balancing work, family, and medical needs. Nearly half of workers in America still lack paid sick leave and are forced to choose between losing the salary they desperately need and jeopardizing their health and the health of those around them. After passing a comprehensive paid sick leave policy, New York City found not only that it improved the health and financial security of workers, but also that unemployment dropped, and businesses grew. According to the Conference of State Legislatures, ten states and the District of Columbia require paid sick leave, but there is no national requirement. Sick and family leave benefits were provided on a temporary basis during the coronavirus pandemic and this should spur a relook at it as a national policy. Congress did pass the Federal Employee Paid Leave Act which just took effect in October 2020 and grants 12 weeks of paid family leave to federal employees for the birth or placement of a child. Some ten States offer various forms of family leave benefit, but national policy is lacking and urgently needed.

- **Expand Earned Income Tax Credits**—The EITC is one of our most effective anti-poverty programs. It provides tax relief to low-income workers to ensure that no one who labors to earn a basic wage is taxed back into poverty. According to the Center on Budget and Policy Priorities, the EITC helped lift 6.2 million people out of poverty in 2013. But the current law overlooks too many workers in need, including those low-income workers without children and workers under twenty-five or over sixty-five. This measure has received bipartisan support.

- **Expand childcare subsidies**—The high cost of quality childcare takes a dramatic toll on low-income families across the country. A report from the Economic Policy Institute found that in every state, quality childcare costs more than 30 percent of a minimum-wage worker's earnings. Access to high-quality childcare allows parents to support their families and better prepares children to learn and grow into healthy adults. We should not ask people to choose between their kids and their paychecks. The primary funding for childcare subsidies is the federal–state Child Care and Development Fund (CCDF). The federal government contributes fixed amounts of funding and provides guidance through CCDF, and states contribute a minimum required level of funding and administer the subsidies, sometimes with the help of localities and private partners. Unfortunately, current funding is only enough to serve about 15 percent of families eligible under federal guidelines.

- **Expand eligibility and opportunity for affordable housing units**—There is a significant shortage of affordable housing units across the country. The Low-Income Housing Tax Credit program, which we used at N Street Village to construct fifty-one affordable rental units, is one important tool to help solve the affordable housing crisis. But analyses suggest the program is falling short of meeting its potential to help poor families move to low-poverty neighborhoods with strong schools and low crime, which research shows can have a range of benefits, including raising children's long-run earnings and chances of attending college. Strategies to deal with homelessness prevalent in many cities include Rapid Re-Housing, Targeted Affordable Housing, Permanent

Supportive Housing, and other strategies discussed earlier in the case study of the Homeward DC plan to end long-term homelessness.

Other social and environmental policies to support the common good

- **Expand affordable health care to all**—Our current patchwork system includes some employer-provided insurance, Medicare for seniors, Medicaid for lower income, and state health exchanges with subsidies up to a certain income. But there are many still falling through the gaps. The 2010 ACA was a critical step toward making sure that all Americans can access the health care they need, but it stopped well short of realizing the goal of universal health access. Health insurance and care is high on the list of political issues in recent elections and will likely continue to be while many are still uncovered and while medical costs continue to rise. Various options toward universal coverage were widely debated in the lead-up to the 2020 elections. Now with the new Biden administration, healthcare policy will be a top priority. If COVID-19 has taught us anything, it is that our health system is in urgent need of repair.
- **Improve education at all levels**—Universal Pre-K has been enacted in some states and should really be a national priority; too many kids are left behind starting at an early age. Regarding public education, various national efforts such as No Child Left Behind and Common Core have been initiated, but still the quality of education seems to have improved relatively little, and we seem to be falling behind other developed countries in math and science.

In the latest test scores, we were not even among the top ten countries. The public-school experience during the pandemic has illustrated the wide inequality in education access, with many low-income students struggling to connect virtually. Regarding postsecondary education, community colleges can be a vital technical training option when coordinated with industry in the region. As mentioned earlier, the American Enterprise Institute presented three case studies of community colleges partnering with the automotive industry to help get students job ready. Others are advocating reduced or free tuition at public colleges, at least for lower-income students.

- **Assure racial equity**— More than a half century ago in 1968, the Kerner Commission report on racial inequities was released. The commission's report concluded that racial unrest at the time was a product of a wide range of injustices, ranging from inadequate schools and housing to poverty-wage jobs and discriminatory treatment from police and the criminal justice system. Unfortunately, rather than address these inequities the nation turned toward law and order and massive imprisonment, particularly of young Black men. In 2020, we sadly witnessed the disproportionate impact of the coronavirus pandemic on minorities followed by multiple high-profile police killings of African Americans which resulted in continuing nationwide protests led by Black Lives Matter (BLM). Major public support has developed for police reform and addressing systemic racism.

- **Assure the right to vote**—The right to vote is such a fundamental right in our country yet the struggle continues. We have seen multiple states try to roll back voter rights by reducing advance polling days and requiring IDs that are not readily available to all, among other tactics. By 2016, the Brennan Law Center had identified fifteen states that had enacted or tried to enact, subject to court challenge, more restrictive voting practices. In addition, gerrymandering in some states has used racial factors to skew congressional districts. In 2017, the Supreme Court, in a significant 5–3 decision written by Justice Elena Kagan, concluded that North Carolina had violated the Equal Protections Clause of the Fourteenth Amendment by separating voters in different districts on the basis of race without "sufficient justification" for doing so. As a result of the coronavirus, most states expanded mail-in ballot options for the 2020 elections. But President Trump and his allies falsely claimed the potential for massive fraud with mail-in-ballots and continually challenged the election results after Biden was declared the winner. The House voted in July 2020 by unanimous consent to approve a measure, proposed by House Majority Whip James Clyburn (D-S.C.) to rename their already passed Voting Rights Act the "John R. Lewis Voting Rights Act." Voting Rights should be an urgent item for the incoming Congress in 2021.

- **Enact immigration reform**—For the millions of people who live in the US without documentation or with only temporary permission to work, finding stable employment can be nearly impossible. Many more immigrants are barred from accessing the social programs they need because of decades of anti-immigrant legislation. By allowing immigrants to come out of the shadows and fully participate in society, immigration reform would benefit individual families and our communities; the

CBO has estimated that immigration reform would reduce our federal budget deficit by $200 billion over ten years. The Border Security, Economic Opportunity, and Immigration Modernization Act in 2013 was a viable solution for fixing our broken immigration system and had been endorsed widely by business and government entities. In June 2013, the Senate passed the bill with a 68–32 margin, and it had the votes to pass the House, but Republican leadership did not allow it to come up for a vote. Unfortunately, a great reform opportunity was missed, and with the election of Donald Trump in 2016, the progress on immigration reform was set back indefinitely. The Trump administration attacked immigrants on multiple fronts, and many activists resisted these policies. Near-term priorities include permanent protection for Dreamers and TPS holders. The incoming Biden Administration is quickly moving on the immigration front by rolling back the so called 'Muslim ban', reinstating DACA provisions, and submitting a comprehensive immigration reform bill to allow a path to citizenship for some 11 million illegal immigrants.

- **Prioritize environmental sustainability**—Climate change increasingly looms as a primary environmental threat to coming generations. Irreversible climate-induced catastrophes are likely in this century and beyond if action is not taken to slow carbon emissions. Foremost among the options is moving toward sustainable energy sources. A relatively new bipartisan Climate Leadership Council including energy companies and environmental groups has proposed a plan for an economy-wide fee on CO_2 emissions, with rebates to all citizens in an attempt to make the program revenue-neutral. The goal is to cut emissions in half by 2035. The incoming Biden administration will likely reverse many of the Trump administration's regressive climate policies and regulations, including weakening of vehicle fuel and emission standards, which were to be a central part of our greenhouse emissions reduction targets in the coming decade. And importantly, the Biden administration just rejoined the Paris climate accord to help lead global climate policy rather than being a tragic solo resister on the global sidelines.

Supporting the Common Good in Public Policy through Community Action

We fortunately have First Amendment protections of speech in the US Constitution: "Congress shall make no law respecting an establishment of religion or prohibiting the free exercise thereof; or abridging the freedom of speech, or of the press; or the right of the people peaceably to assemble, and to petition the government for a redress of grievances." One of our nation's founders, Thomas Jefferson, posed this question: "If you had to choose between having a government or a working press, which would you choose?" He came down clearly on the side of the press. Governments, he reasoned, can do sinister, self-serving things with no watchdogs around. But the press, he felt, was that watchdog, the eyes and ears of the people, a source for honest information sharing. Jefferson further said that, "Our citizens may be deceived for a while…but as long as the presses can be protected, we may trust to them for light…Whenever the people are well-informed, they can be trusted with their own government."

Freedom of speech is not limited to speaking, writing, or rallying; it also protects symbolic actions of resistance such as students or athletes wearing armbands or kneeling in resistance during the playing of the national anthem or even acts of desecration of the flag. And of course, political protesters exercising free speech have the right to picket, to distribute literature, to chant, and to engage passersby in debate, but protesters can be limited by government from certain actions, such as blocking building entrances or occupying designated security zones. But protesting in these prohibited spaces is often done intentionally to force arrest as a symbolic act of resistance.

We are in a period when resistance is a must when our democracy is threatened. It is a time to reflect on the words of Robert Kennedy: "Every time we turn our heads the other way when we see the law flouted, when we tolerate

> The former slave and leading abolitionist **Frederick Douglass** once wrote:
>
> "I prayed for freedom for twenty years, but received no answer, until I prayed with my legs."

what we know to be wrong, when we close our eyes and ears to the corrupt because we are too busy or too frightened, when we fail to speak up and speak out, we strike a blow against freedom and decency and justice." Benjamin Franklin once said, "Justice will not be served until those who are unaffected are as outraged as those who are." James Baldwin said about speaking out, "I love America more than any other country in this world, and, exactly for this reason, I insist on the right to criticize her perpetually"; and he said in regard to social engagement, "Not everything that is faced can be changed, but nothing can be changed until it is faced." The great abolitionist of the 19th century, the former slave Frederick Douglass, wrote: "I prayed for freedom for twenty years, but received no answer, until I prayed with my legs."

History suggests that successful resistance movements need the support of a permanent infrastructure, and they must be willing to engage in the time-intensive organizing that changes minds and behavior. It is instructive to look at some historic examples of resistance to shed light on what might be needed today. The case of the abolitionist movement is a key example. During the administration of another populist president, Andrew Jackson, who was proslavery, a resistance movement began. In 1831, William Lloyd Garrison and friends he called the "Twelve Apostles" met in a Black church (no white one would have them) and signed the charter of the New England Anti-Slavery Society. Theirs was the first of what would be thousands of such societies, which were highly organized. They elected executive committees to run their affairs, dispatched speakers to spread the word, and held annual conventions. Abolitionists built momentum through speeches, books, essays, pamphlets, and other activities to change public opinion.

Then, of course, the Underground Railroad emerged, in which many abolitionists risked their lives over subsequent decades to save thousands of people who had run away from their enslavers. Harriet Tubman, a runaway slave in eastern Maryland, whose figure is represented on a stained-glass window in our church, became perhaps the best-known of all the Underground Railroad's "conductors." During a ten-year span, she made nineteen trips into the South and escorted more than three hundred enslaved people to freedom. And as she once proudly pointed out to Frederick Douglass, an antislavery orator, in all her journeys she "never lost a single passenger." Frederick Douglass said, "Slavery is not abolished until the Black man has the ballot," and although the Fifteenth Amendment to the Constitution was ratified in 1870, it would not be until a hundred years later that the Voting Rights Act of 1965 would really implement that right! And unfortunately, there are still state legislatures trying to constrain that right through mechanisms such as voter ID restrictions and gerrymandering, which disproportionately affect Blacks and other minorities.

The 1954 US Supreme Court decision *Brown v. Board of Education of Topeka, Kansas* helped usher in a new era in the struggle for civil rights. This landmark decision outlawed racial segregation in public schools and led to the largest social resistance movement of the twentieth century in the United States. The movement broadened to include at least three areas of discrimination: education, social segregation, and voting rights. Some say the civil rights movement was effectively launched with the arrest of seamstress Rosa Parks in Montgomery, Alabama, for refusing to give up her seat to a white man on a Montgomery city bus in 1955. After the arrest, Blacks throughout the city joined together in a massive rally outside one of the city's Baptist churches to hear the young preacher Martin Luther King Jr. speak out against segregation. Blacks also organized the Montgomery bus boycott, boycotting city transportation for nearly a year before the Supreme Court finally struck down the city's segregated bus seating as unconstitutional. The civil rights movement led by Dr. Martin Luther King Jr. was a largely nonviolent movement in the tradition of Gandhi. It also influenced the subsequent women's rights movement, the student movement of the 1960s, and the Vietnam war protests extending into the 1970s.

Later, in the early years of the twenty-first century, "Freedom to Marry" activists developed a smart approach to same-sex marriage rights. For example, they trained supporters to each have conversations with five of their friends or relatives—and to ask people who responded positively to seek out five more. Further, in 2012, they decided to support ballot fights in Maine, Minnesota, Washington, and Maryland. Those states all ended up backing marriage equality and gave significant momentum to the cause. One factor that helped was changing the message from one of rights to one of desire for love and commitment, giving a more personal face to same-sex marriage.

This is something immigration activists have recently tried to do, by making young immigrants—the DACA recipients or "Dreamers"—the human face of their movement. Policies of the Trump administration, including repeal of DACA, mass deportation, and separation of families, have reignited immigration activists. Many faith communities went into action to help DACA recipients, TPS holders, families caught up in the massive deportation approach, and refugees. Sanctuary is one tool that has religious roots in the Judeo-Christian tradition. In the Old Testament, God commanded Moses to set aside cities and places of refuge in Canaan where the persecuted could seek asylum. And in the Christian tradition Jesus emphasized ministering to the "least of these," including the stranger among us. These biblical ideas have been embraced by historical movements, from the Underground Railroad during slavery in the US to the efforts to provide sanctuary to Jews during World War II, to the large sanctuary movement during the 1980s that sought to protect Central American refugees from war-torn countries.

Unfortunately, a generation of young people are now witnessing what they do not want for the future direction of our country, and they are leading several resistance movements. For example, in August 2018, sixteen-year-old Greta Thunberg started a school strike for the climate outside the Swedish

Parliament that has since spread all over the world and now involves more than 100,000 schoolchildren. This is a good example of the new era of organizing that Dana Fisher discusses in her new book, *American Resistance*, which she describes as "distributed organizing, that focuses not on geographic location or pre-existing social ties, but rather on digital connections." The Women's March in January 2017, which she analyzes in her book, is a key example of the relatively new digital organizing that quickly mobilized people throughout the country in resistance. The result was the largest protest movement in history, and Fisher reports that a third of the people who protested that day were new to organized resistance and that they remain active; this is encouraging to hear because we certainly need resistance at this time in our history.

Pope Francis in his October 2020 encyclical reflects that the struggle is long and, "each new generation must take up the struggles and attainments of past generations, while setting its sights even higher. This is the path. Goodness, together with love, justice, and solidarity, are not achieved once and for all; they have to be realized each day. It is not possible to settle for what was achieved in the past and complacently enjoy it, as if we could somehow disregard the fact that many of our brothers and sisters still endure situations that cry out for our attention."

And now, as I conclude my book in early 2021, we sadly have witnessed the disproportionate impact of the coronavirus pandemic on minorities followed by multiple high-profile police killings of African Americans which resulted in nationwide protests led by Black Lives Matter against racism, and finally the tragic attack on the nation's Capitol by white supremacists encouraged by a President claiming a stolen election. This is all still unfolding as I conclude my book, but it is clear that we have entered another period in our history where active resistance in the streets is leading us to reflect and act on systemic racism in so many parts of our society. With new national leadership in place, many hope that we are entering a positive era of change that will bring and end to COVID-19 suffering, more economic equality, racial healing, and action to stem climate change.

Examples of Social Justice Movements in American History

Abolitionist movement—As mentioned earlier, the abolitionist movement to end slavery in the US started formally in 1831 with William Lloyd Garrison, a journalist and social reformer, and friends he called the Twelve Apostles. Garrison founded an anti-slavery newspaper entitled *The Liberator.* Frederick Douglass, who escaped slavery himself, was also an instrumental figure in the abolitionist movement as well as an advocate for women's suffrage. Abolitionists relied on the power of books, essays, pamphlets, speeches, and other activities, all with the goal of changing people's minds. By 1840 there were an estimated 15,000 abolitionist members. Although Black and white abolitionists often worked together, by the 1840s they differed in philosophy and method. While many white abolitionists focused almost exclusively on slavery, Black Americans tended to couple anti-slavery activities with demands for racial equality and justice.

Women's suffrage movement—Elizabeth Cady Stanton, Susan B. Anthony, and Lucretia Mott spearheaded the strong push for equal voting rights for women in the mid-nineteenth century. After the Seneca Falls Convention in 1848, the rallying cry for women's right to vote would not be suppressed. With the Constitutional amendments regarding slavery and civil rights in the late 1860s, many former abolitionists took up the cause of women's suffrage and applied lessons learned from their earlier movement. The so-called Silent Sentinels conducted a nonviolent protest outside the White House in 1919, and this was to be the culminating event that led to the right to vote for women. In 1920—forty-one years after it had originally been drafted—Congress ratified an amendment that said, "The right of citizens of the United States to vote shall not be denied or abridged by the United States or by any State on account of sex."

Labor movement—The labor movement in the United States grew out of the need to protect the interests of workers during the Industrial Revolution. The Catholic Worker Movement led by Dorothy Day was instrumental in mobilizing the labor movement. Organized labor unions fought for better wages, reasonable hours, and safer working conditions and led efforts to stop child labor, give health benefits, and provide injury and retirement benefits. By the end of World War II, more than 12 million workers belonged to unions, and collective bargaining had taken hold throughout the industrial economy. Unfortunately, unionization has declined over the decades since as have working class incomes.

Civil rights movement—Two key moments in the long struggle for civil rights for African Americans, Rosa Parks' refusal to give up a seat on the bus in Alabama in 1955 and the March on Washington on August 28, 1963, when more than 200,000 people descended on Washington, DC, proved that protests do not need to be violent to be powerful. In addition to meeting

> **Rosa Parks** said about giving up her seat on the bus on that fateful day in Montgomery in 1955:
>
> "I had been pushed around all my life and felt at that moment that I couldn't take it anymore"

with President John F. Kennedy and members of Congress, the groups' leaders led a march from the Washington Monument to the Lincoln Memorial. The gathered masses stood peaceably for hours in the stifling summer heat as civil rights leaders appealed for equal rights for African Americans and, more broadly, all minorities. Thanks to powerful words from these prominent leaders, including Martin Luther King Jr.'s famed "I Have a Dream" speech, the march went down in history as the most convincing event in the movement that led to the successful passage of the Civil Rights Act of 1964, the Voting Rights Act of 1965, and more.

Vietnam War protests—The Vietnam anti-war movement brought out younger activists for the first time; they were, of course, the ones subject to the draft, and they resisted because so many believed that the war was a mistake and that the government was distorting the truth about the progress of the ill-conceived war. With no clear sign of impending victory in Vietnam, the daily media images of American military casualties helped to stimulate opposition to the war more broadly in America. In the frigid fall of 1969, more than 500,000 people marched on Washington to protest US involvement in the Vietnam War. It was one of the largest political rallies in the nation's history. The growing opposition to the United States' involvement in the Vietnam War led to its eventual end. It also ended the career of President Johnson, as he withdrew from reelection in March 1970 in the face of stiff opposition to his support for the war.

The Poor People's Campaign—In 1968, Rev. Dr. Martin Luther King Jr. and many others called for a "revolution of values" in America. They sought to build a broad movement that could unite poor and affected communities across the country. The name chosen, "The Poor People's Campaign," was intended to reflect a movement that was concerned with lifting up those who were marginalized. Today, the Poor People's Campaign: A National Call for Moral Revival has picked up this unfinished work, believing we are in a moral crisis not unlike 1968, the year of the initial campaign. The group organized a multistate movement that led into the Mass Poor People's Assembly and Moral March on Washington, when thousands connected virtually on June 20, 2020, to demonstrate the power of the movement and call for action. The movement calls for implementation of a broad moral agenda and calls people of conscience to engage in deeply moral civic engagement and voting that cares about poor and low-wealth people, the sick, immigrants, workers, the environment, people with disabilities, the LGBTQ community, and peace over war.

Environmental movement—On the birth of Earth Day, April 22, 1970, 20 million Americans took to the streets to demonstrate for a healthy, sustainable environment. Earth Day 1970 achieved a rare bipartisan alignment, enlisting wide support from both Republicans and Democrats. The movement led to the creation of the Environmental Protection Agency in 1970 and the passage of major environmental legislation. Earth Day is now the largest secular observance in the world, celebrated by more than a billion people, and 2020 marked the fiftieth anniversary of the day.

Climate change has become an increasing focus of the environmental movement. In September 2019, leading up to the UN climate conference in New York, young people from around the world led a massive, coordinated strike from school on Friday, September 20, to protest government and business inaction on climate change. It was one of the largest environmental protests in history and had as its leader a sixteen-year-old climate activist from Sweden, Greta Thunberg. This led to the Fridays for Future movement, which conducted climate protest rallies in many cities throughout the fall of 2019. In December 2019, Greta Thunberg was selected by *Time* magazine as its Person of the Year.

Gay rights—In 1993, over 800,000 people marched on the Mall in DC for the rights of the gay community, in more recent times referred to as the LGBTQ (and recently added IA) community. They were seeking laws that would protect citizens from discrimination based on sexual identity and an increase in funding for AIDS research. That march and subsequent mobilizations and litigations helped gain national social recognition for the LGBTQ community. After decades of activists building momentum for change, on June 26, 2015, the US Supreme Court struck down all state bans on same-sex marriage, legalized it in all fifty states, and required states to honor out-of-state same-sex marriage licenses. And importantly, the Supreme Court ruled in June 2020 that civil rights law protects gay and transgender workers from workplace discrimination.

#MeToo movement—The #MeToo movement was born out of long-standing gender inequities and increased focus on sexual harassment in politics, boardrooms, and newsrooms, with numerous allegations and prominent media firings. A tipping point was reached in recent years with high-profile examples such as Harvey Weinstein. This movement is helping thousands of women come forward who might have been too intimidated in the past to go public alone. The day after Trump's inauguration in January 2017, the Women's March became one of the largest demonstrations in American history, drawing together hundreds of thousands of women from across the country, along with the men who supported them, to protest gender oppression. They called again for the Equal Rights Amendment to be included in the Constitution, and the amendment gained new life recently as Virginia finally passed it in January 2020 under the new Democratic legislature. March participants emphasized issues like affordable childcare, pay equality, job discrimination, sexual harassment, and a women's right to choose. Following the exposure of the widespread sexual-abuse allegations against Harvey Weinstein in October 2017, the movement began to spread virally as a hashtag on social media and helped empower other women to come forward regarding sexual abuse they had experienced in their lives. Women have also increasingly sought elected office in recent years with a record number running for Congress in 2020.

Black Lives Matter- BlackLivesMatter (BLM) was founded in 2013 in response to the acquittal of Trayvon Martin's killer. In 2020, BLM led nationwide protests for police defunding and reform trigged by the killing of George Floyd by Minneapolis police officers. The movement seems to have become embedded in the mainstream in ways that would have been unthinkable just a few years ago. Americans have turned out for what some are calling the most sweeping and sustained protests in the country's history. A 2020 documentary on Congressman John Lewis who recently died takes its name from one of his favorite phrases, "good trouble." Lewis often said, "Never, ever be afraid to make some noise and get in good trouble, necessary trouble." He is referring to his belief in nonviolent protest and disobedience. As one of the student leaders of the civil-rights movement, Lewis was arrested some 40 times for demonstrations that included marching with King from Selma to Montgomery. His last public outing was to visit BLM Plaza in DC near the White House in June 2020.

BLM Plaza image in DC near the White House

Community Organizing for Justice

Community organizing is a strategy to bring about social change that improves the quality of community life. Community organizing brings people together around their shared interests to form bonds that empower them to take action to improve their communities. This is often done through coalitions of faith communities, as has been my experience in the Washington, DC, metropolitan area, but there are good secular examples also. In her recent book *Who Do We Choose to Be? Facing Reality, Claiming Leadership, Restoring Sanity*, Margaret J. Wheatley says,

> It is possible, in this time of profound disruption, for leadership to be a noble profession that contributes to the "common good" … It is possible to find a path of contribution and meaning if we turn our attention away from issues beyond our control and focus on the people around us who are yearning for good leadership and engage them in work that is within reach. It is possible to use our influence and power to create "islands of sanity" in the midst of a raging destructive sea. So much is possible if we consciously and wisely choose how best to step forward as leaders for this time.

We clearly need islands of sanity in our times as so much chaos has been sown around us, even by our national leaders.

An early community organizer, although she was not referred to as such, was Dorothy Day. She helped found the Catholic Worker Movement and its publication the *Catholic Worker*, which inspired the movement. Over several decades, the *Catholic Worker* attracted such writers and editors as Michael Harrington, Thomas Merton, and Daniel Berrigan. The movement also created a shelter that provided food and clothing to the poor of the Lower East Side and then a series of farms for communal living. Beginning in 1935, the *Catholic Worker* began publishing articles that articulated a rigorous and uncompromising pacifist position, breaking with the traditional Catholic doctrine of just war theory. The movement quickly spread to other cities in the United States and to Canada and the United Kingdom.

Saul Alinsky, based in Chicago, is credited with originating the term "community organizer" and published books such as *Rules for Radicals* to codify key strategies and aims of community organizing. Training and support organizations for national coalitions of mostly locally governed and faith-based community organizing groups were founded in the Alinsky tradition. The Industrial Areas Foundation was the first, created by Alinsky himself in 1940. Faith in Action is another such organization. Community organizing examples in the Washington, DC, metro area are discussed in the following paragraphs, along with an example from Rwanda; I have personally been involved in most of these.

The **Washington Interfaith Network** (WIN) in DC is a broad-based, multiracial, multi-faith, strictly nonpartisan, District-wide citizens' power organization. Rooted in local congregations and associations, WIN has been operating for over twenty years. It grew out of the Industrial Areas Foundation network started by Saul Alinsky in Chicago. WIN is committed to training and developing neighborhood leaders, to addressing community issues, and to holding elected and corporate officials accountable in Washington, DC. WIN seeks to create long-term power through a broad and united front of organized institutions, organized people, and organized money—acting consistently and persistently for change on multiple issues at the neighborhood, regional, national, and citywide levels. It has been most active on issues of homelessness, affordable housing, jobs, transportation, and immigration. The base of the organization is the hundreds of leaders building and maintaining strong relationships through congregations, social service organizations, and other community organizations. Training for action is an important part of WIN; I personally participated in one of their three-day intensive training sessions and witnessed the power of one-on-one relationship-building techniques and techniques of advocacy for institutional change.

Congregation Action Network (CAN) formed in the last few years in the Washington metro area to provide support and solidarity to neighbors, friends, and family who fear being detained, deported, or profiled and to engage in advocacy and protest of detrimental governmental policies. It is supported by Faith in Action, a national community organizing entity. Some CAN congregations are hosting or otherwise supporting people who are at risk of deportation; others are accompanying people to immigration agency check-ins and legal hearings, holding Defend Your Rights trainings, setting up rapid-response networks to show up when ICE raids take place, and pressing local governments to get ICE out of schools, jails, and courts and end policies that racially profile and over-incarcerate people of color. CAN has also been active in support of DACA and TPS recipients. When COVID-19 emerged, a group of volunteers affiliated with CAN created an all-volunteer organizing collective to support immigrants and other marginalized communities in the metro DC area. Called the Food Justice Initiative, the team initiated a campaign to distribute food resources to folks in the community and over the subsequent months distributed food to thousands of families.

**Immigration advocates question Senate Majority Leader
Schumer at Supreme Court DACA protest June 2020**

The new **Poor People's Campaign** was launched in DC in May 2018 by Reverend William Barber of North Carolina, fifty years after Martin Luther King Jr.'s original Poor People's Campaign, with a march on the Capitol and civil disobedience. The campaign continued with Moral Monday protests at the Capitol, which Rev. Barber also led for many years at the statehouse in North Carolina. On June 20, 2020, the campaign conducted a national virtual event as they were unable to have a culminating march and demonstration at the Capitol due to COVID-19. The event leaders called for the implementation of a moral agenda that cares about the poor and weakest in our society. Many faith communities, including my own, have been engaged with the movement in DC.

In northern Virginia, an organization called **Social Action Linking Together** (SALT) is a network of over 1,200 persons embracing the principle that "the justice of a society can be measured by how the most vulnerable members of that society are faring and being treated." SALT includes individual volunteers from various faith communities and secular organizations. These individuals and faith communities are in solidarity with one another as a network of advocates dedicated to advancing justice and the common good. SALT members propose and shape fair public social policies through education of policy makers and advocacy work.

Mutual Aid Movement DC, housed at Luther Place church, is a community-based entity composed of grassroots volunteers and service workers providing food and other supplies to needy families and seniors during the pandemic and beyond. Mutual aid as a concept is "cooperation for the sake of the common good." It brings people together to help meet each other's needs for the benefit of the whole community. Mutual Aid is a practice that emphasizes solidarity rather than charity and recognizes that well-being, health, and dignity are all bound up in each other and that our survival depends on cooperation, not competition.

I have personally witnessed community organizing in **Rwanda,** a country devastated by genocide just twenty-five years ago. Rwanda is now advancing socially and economically faster than most other African countries. Our friend there, Pastor John Rutsindintwarane, who is skilled in community organizing, has been working with many local rural communities over the last fourteen years to identify their most pressing community needs and then helping them organize to get things done. For Pastor John, the devastating effects of the 1994 genocide and the overwhelming challenges faced by the survivors fueled his commitment to try new approaches, combining faith with action and rebuilding at the local community level. He began his work in a remote part of southeastern Rwanda, Mumeya, where residents lacked many public services. He offered his help to organize the local community, to address their most critical problems. Mumeya villagers from five different congregations began leadership training under a tree in the village. Soon, community leaders began holding one-to-one conversations to identify the major needs in the community. After hundreds of these conversations took place, residents decided that a health center was their top priority. I personally visited the Mumeya village in August 2006 and heard the residents express their dream of a medical clinic for the village. At that time, all that they had to show was a pile of rocks that would form the foundation of the clinic. For the next three years, they organized their own labor and resources and gained supplies and medical staff from public officials, and in 2009, after completion of three rooms, they opened their health center.

Since then, Mumeyans have formed partnerships with local and national governments to secure more than $6 million in improvements and services, including access to water and electricity, new roads, and two new public schools. Over the past decade, organizing has spread to other districts across Rwanda. Projects include health clinics, water, electricity, three schools, a community center, new homes, reforestation, and road construction. In the picture below, local women lead another rural community near Nyarubuye in building a much-needed medical clinic. This community was devastated by the 1994 genocide when thousands were killed in the local Catholic Church.

**Local women lead rural Rwanda community near
Nyarubuye in building a medical clinic.**

I close this section on activism by quoting Teddy Roosevelt:

> It is not the critic who counts; not the person who points out how the strong person stumbles, or where the doer of deeds could have done them better. The credit belongs to the person who is actually in the arena, whose face is marred by dust and sweat and blood; who strives valiantly; who errs, who comes short again and again, because there is no effort without error and shortcoming; but who does actually strive to do the deeds; who knows great enthusiasms, the great devotions; who spends himself/herself in a worthy cause; who at the best knows in the end the triumph of high achievement, and who at the worst, if he fails, at least fails while daring greatly, so that his/her place shall never be with those cold and timid souls who neither know victory nor defeat.

10
Concluding Thoughts

One of the great issues of our time is the crisis of the common good, the sense of community solidarity that binds all in a common destiny. Theologian Walter Brueggemann says in his book *Journey to the Common Good*, "We face a crisis about the common good because there are powerful forces at work among us to resist the common good, to violate community solidarity, and to deny a common destiny. Mature people, at their best, are people committed to the common good that reaches beyond private interest, transcends sectarian commitments, and offers human solidarity." David Brooks, in his recent book *The Second Mountain: The Quest for a Moral Life*, addresses the commitments that define a life of meaning and purpose, including family, vocation, and community. Brooks critiques the excesses of "hyper-individualism" while urging reflection and action through purpose beyond one's self. He builds on other authors in recent decades who worry that individualism has grown "cancerous" and is destroying the social fabric of our nation and communities. Further, Peter Wehner, a conservative columnist for the New York Times, says in his recent book, *The Death of Politics: How to Heal Our Frayed Republic after Trump*, that "civility is central to citizenship." He suggests that without civility everything in life becomes a battlefield, and families, communities, and institutions can break apart. Importantly, we need leadership that can bring the nation together in these difficult times. What the country witnessed during COVID-19 has sadly demonstrated the effects of poor national leadership.

I have been fortunate to be involved for much of my life in interfaith community action following the biblical tenets of welcoming the stranger, the outcast, the excluded of society. Out of that understanding, my church, Luther Place, took the bold act of opening the doors of the church to the homeless in the particularly cold winter of 1976, when many were dying. Out of that action of welcoming the stranger emerged the miracle of N Street Village, a continuum of programs for homeless women that now serves nearly two thousand women annually at multiple locations in Washington, DC as discussed earlier. Also, in the late 1970s, the Luther Place community welcomed refugees from the conflict in Vietnam. In the 1980s, when we saw many refugees from wars in Central America, our church, among many others, provided sanctuary for those immigrants facing persecution at home. This was the way the US acted through much of its history, and I am confident it will again rise above today's ugly expressions of bigotry and xenophobia. Unfortunately, too much of Christianity (the so-called religious right) today has bought into demagoguery and often aligns itself with the forces of bigotry.

At Luther Place, we have four great witnesses to reform and justice on the front stained-glass windows of the sanctuary: Martin Luther, Dr. Martin Luther King Jr., Dietrich Bonhoeffer, and Harriet Tubman. We chose these four witnesses during a renovation in the late 1990s. After much debate, we settled on these four, of all the great reformers and justice seekers, to represent our vision. Martin Luther was the great reformer of a corrupt religious system who brought the language and the gospel to the masses some five hundred years ago in Germany.

Dr. Martin Luther King Jr. led the great civil rights movement of the 1960s, culminating in major civil rights legislation such as the Civil Rights Act of 1964 and the Voting Rights Act of 1965. Dietrich Bonhoeffer was a German Lutheran theologian who gave his life in resistance to the evil Nazi regime. Finally, Harriet Tubman, who escaped enslavement, helped lead hundreds out of slavery through the Underground Railroad. An additional remarkable justice leader, Dorothy Day of the Catholic Worker Movement, is also prominently pictured on a door mural on the exterior of our church.

Their remarkable stories are elaborated below:

Martin Luther: Luther is one of the more influential figures in Western history. His writings and actions were responsible for sparking the Protestant Reformation in parallel with the Renaissance. His translation of the Bible into German (from Latin) made it much more accessible to the laity, which had a tremendous impact on both the church and German culture and fostered the development of a standard version of the German language. Facilitated by the emergence of the printing press, his liberating writings became available to the masses. Unfortunately, later in life, Luther expressed antagonistic views toward Jews in his writings. These statements and their influence on anti-Semitism have been widely condemned in faith communities and beyond.

Dr. Martin Luther King Jr: It has been more than half a century since Martin Luther King Jr.'s death, but his vision provides lasting ideals of the common good. As mentioned earlier, one of Dr. King's most compelling visions was that of a "beloved community," in which he envisioned a society based on justice (both economic and social), equal opportunity, and love of one's fellow human beings and one in which we would peacefully march ahead together for a more just society. King offered us hope in his prophetic "Mountaintop" speech the night before his asassination in Memphis, saying that there would be difficult days ahead but that he was comforted, having seen the Promised Land from the moutaintop.

Dietrich Bonhoeffer: Bonhoeffer was a German Lutheran theologian who actively resisted white nationalism under the Hitler regime, which eventually cost him his life. He wrote *The Cost of Discipleship* (1937), a call to more faithful and radical obedience to the message of the gospel and a rebuke of comfortable Christianity. Unfortunately, the Catholic Church and the mainline Protestant churches were enabling of Hitler, in what was to be a pact with the devil. Bonhoeffer observed that there were three classes of individuals in that time of crisis: the perpetrators, the bystanders, and the protesters. The Nazis, of course, were the perpetrators; the institutional church and much of the populace were bystanders; and Bonhoeffer and colleagues were to become the protesters or resisters. Bonhoeffer helped organize an alternative Confessing Church in opposition to Nazis and taught pastors in an underground seminary. But after the seminary was discovered and closed, the Confessing Church became increasingly reluctant to speak out against Hitler, so Bonhoeffer began to change his strategy. To this point he had been a pacifist, and he had tried to oppose the Nazis through religious action and moral persuasion. He then took a risky step and signed up with the German secret service, to act as a double agent—while traveling to church conferences over Europe, he was supposed to be collecting information about the places he visited, but he was instead trying to help Jews escape Nazi oppression. Bonhoeffer also became part of a plot to overthrow, and later to try to assassinate, Hitler. He was discovered by the

Nazis and was hanged in 1945, only weeks before the Allies overthrew Hitler.

Harriet Tubman: Born into slavery in Maryland, Harriet Tubman escaped to freedom in the North in 1849 and became the most famous "conductor" on the Underground Railroad. Tubman risked her life to lead hundreds of family members and other enslaved people from the plantation system to freedom via this elaborate secret network of safe houses. Tubman became so well-known for leading slaves to freedom that she was called the "Moses of Her People." Already a leading abolitionist before the Civil War, Tubman also helped the Union Army during the war, working as a spy among other roles. After the Civil War ended, Tubman dedicated her life to helping impoverished former slaves and the elderly. In honor of her life and by popular demand, in 2016 the US Treasury Department announced that Harriet Tubman will eventually replace Andrew Jackson on the center of a new $20 bill.

> **Harriet Tubman:** "Every great dream begins with a dreamer. Always remember, you have within you the strength, the patience, and the passion to reach for the stars to change the world."

Dorothy Day: Dorothy Day founded the *Catholic Worker* newspaper in 1933 and served as its editor until her death in 1980. She wrote about the conditions of poor people and especially about the conditions of workers and the labor movement, which was struggling for recognition. She sought to synthesize Catholic social teaching in such a way that it would inspire volunteers and clergy. Out of this initiative also grew the Catholic Worker Movement; Catholic workers joined street protests and labor pickets, helped with the housing and

> **Dorothy Day:** "Don't call me a Saint; I don't want to be dismissed so easily."

feeding of strikers, and called for boycotts of stores where low wages or poor working conditions existed. The movement spread across the United States in the 1930s, and in 1935, Day created the first of many houses of hospitality in New York and other cities. The Catholic Workers set up houses of hospitality where they lived in solidarity with the poor, sick, and homeless people who came to them. The houses served as homeless shelters, community centers, soup kitchens, and prayer gathering spaces.

Another justice seeker I want to highlight is Mahatma Gandhi. He has profound wisdom for our perilous situation today. As most know, he inspired King and other civil rights leaders, and his wisdom is just as helpful today. Here are but a few quotes:

- "All the religions of the world, while they may differ in other respects, unitedly proclaim that nothing lives in this world but Truth."
- "My religion is based on truth and non-violence. Truth is my God. Non-violence is the means of realizing Him."
- "Nonviolence in its dynamic condition means conscious suffering. It does not mean meek submission to the will of the evildoer, but it means the putting of one's whole soul against the will of the tyrant."

Gandhi's focus on "Truth" rings especially strong today as we endured an era of "alternative facts," where we have seen leaders regularly distorting the truth and attacking the free press. Gandhi said that institutions alone cannot protect us; we also need strong moral leaders. He implied that we need truth-telling leaders of high moral character with commitment to public service and to the common good to guide our institutions.

Unfortunately, in recent times we have witnessed leaders who attacked our institutions of government, threatened a free press, and targeted the vulnerable in society. He advises in such situations that individuals and faith communities, secure in their own moral character and community contributions, engage in nonviolent resistance against such demagoguery, untruths, and injustice.

On March 24, 2020, the fortieth anniversary of the assassination of Archbishop Oscar Romero in El Salvador, there were worldwide remembrances of his life. Romero offered people comfort and courage in a particularly dark moment for that country. He openly confronted the country's murderous junta and rejected foreign intervention by the United States. He demanded accountability for the wave of torture and disappearances and stood with the poor and vulnerable against the wealthy and powerful. He was a hero to the vulnerable, but others, including some bishops within the church, accused him of being a communist subversive, driven by politics instead of faith. Thirty-eight years later, Romero was elevated to sainthood in October 2018. At the ceremony, Pope Francis wore the blood-stained rope belt worn by Archbishop Romero when he was murdered in 1980 in front of his worshippers. In his homily, the pope said that Archbishop Romero had "left the security of the world, even his own safety, in order to give his life according to the Gospel, close to the poor and to his people."

When Pope Francis addressed the US Congress in 2015 as part of his visit, he set this challenge to our nation and its leadership: "I am convinced that we can make a difference, and I have no doubt that the United States—and this Congress—have an important role to play. Now is the time for courageous actions and strategies, aimed at implementing a culture of care and an integrated approach to combating poverty, restoring dignity to the excluded, and at the same time protecting nature." After calling for Congress to work for the common good of the people, he sent a prophetic message by going directly to lunch with the homeless, and while with them, he said there was "no moral justification" for their plight. In visiting the homeless, the Pope was following the example of his namesake, Francis of Assisi,

> **Nelson Mandela:** "What counts in life is not the mere fact that we have lived. It is what difference we have made to the lives of others that will determine the significance of the life we lead."

who gave up his wealth and went to serve among the poor. Nelson Mandela said, "What counts in life is not the mere fact that we have lived. It is what difference we have made to the lives of others that will determine the significance of the life we lead."

Many are worried that the future of liberal democracy is seriously threatened. Western democracies, including our own, are facing the biggest challenge since World War II according to Yascha Mounk in his book, *The People vs. Democracy*. He says, "A quarter century ago, most citizens of liberal democracies were very satisfied with their governments ... now they are more disillusioned than they have ever been." Political discord in traditional democratic societies such as the US and UK are only two examples of divisive populist trends. Also, Eastern Europe is seeing a disturbing populist trend back toward authoritarianism.

Economic inequality has contributed significantly to the splintering we are seeing both domestically and internationally. More and more jobs are becoming vulnerable to technology and other global forces; companies are shedding full-time labor and replacing those workers with contract and/or part-time employees. Further, robotics and other technologies are replacing employees. It is estimated that almost 60 percent of the US labor force is paid an hourly wage rather than a salary, and these workers are increasingly responsible for their own pensions and other benefits. Further, salaries and wages have been relatively stagnant over recent decades in real terms; without wage growth, faith in the system diminishes. The US economy produces roughly a third more now than in 1998, yet the labor force has grown little. Further, income inequality has been exacerbated as working-class jobs in manufacturing have been eliminated. Those in advanced technology fields are doing very well, while many others must settle for lower-paying service sector jobs. In the US, economic disparities among regions are certainly driving some of the populism. Cities, primarily coastal, with their more educated workforces, are becoming more prosperous, while other interior, more rural regions have been declining. The thriving regions by and large voted for Hillary Clinton in 2016 and Joe Biden in 2020, while the lagging regions voted heavily for Donald Trump in both elections. Addressing this urban/rural economic disparity and political split will be a key challenge for the incoming Biden Administration.

I have discussed many of these policies in this book that could lead toward the common good. Addressing the increased concentration of income and wealth has to be a key priority along with racial equity. We need improved and affordable education, from Pre-K through college. A well-trained workforce is vital, and one key strategy mentioned is support for community colleges and vocational programs in cooperation with industry. Immigration is certainly a divisive issue, and governments need to be sensitive to emerging concerns and seek reform, but it is imperative that we have immigrants given our nation's aging society and low labor force growth. In light of the devastating impacts of the coronavirus, we need even more urgently to finally move toward universal health care and assure that other critical economic and social benefits are available to all. And importantly, it is urgent that we recommit to stemming climate change.

Looking Ahead

The current divisiveness in America makes it harder than usual for many to feel optimistic about our country. We need a new political paradigm of cooperation for the common good, and as highlighted in earlier chapters, there are many working in community to help build a more inclusive society. We must build on the core principles that truly do make America great; those principles embrace freedom and equality and include an appreciation of the intrinsic worth of every human being. We recognize that our nation has never fully lived up to those principles. But there is a reason immigrants and refugees from around the world still seek their future here—because even now, the United States is still seen as a beacon of liberty around the world, a place where our nation's founding values and rights ultimately triumph. It is in this hope that we must rededicate ourselves to ensure our founding principles are always there for all Americans.

The economic and social turmoil associated with the COVID-19 virus only makes it more urgent that we seek cooperation toward the common good. It has also reminded us that science and professional expertise are important in our lives. During the pandemic, the country has looked to medical experts such as Dr. Anthony Fauci of the National Institutes of Health to understand the threat we were facing. This crisis and its resolution through wide vaccine inoculation hopefully will return Americans toward the idea that government and science are matters for serious and knowledgeable people and that we have a common interest in the well-being of all. We have been most successful when government, civic, and private-sector leaders joined their strengths together in pursuit of the common good. Further, we need to reject an "America First" foreign policy; instead, we need to return to multilateral diplomacy and to the understanding that international cooperation is especially necessary when it comes to dealing with global problems like climate change and viral pandemics.

The COVID-19 crisis has painfully shown that the nation's tattered social safety net is badly in need of repair. Americans need full and reliable access to health care. Americans need affordable childcare and affordable and reliable care of older members of an aging society. No one, especially not children, should ever go hungry, and everyone deserves a place to call home.

In the end, I remain optimistic that through our governmental institutions, laws, courts, elected officials, shared values, and citizen engagement, we can build a better nation and world. We hope for a nation touched "by the better angels of our nature" as Lincoln envisioned. Jon Meacham suggests in his book *The Soul of America: The Battle for Our Better Angels* that *"Our better angels"* reside in that part of the American soul that inspired progressive periods of social reform like the Square Deal, the New Deal, and the Great Society discussed herein. These important examples of our better angels can be the building blocks to a better future for all Americans. When President Joe Biden announced he was running for president, he declared, "We are in the battle for the soul of this nation." Dr. Martin Luther King, Jr. reminded us that progress toward justice is not inevitable and that it often requires long struggles by dedicated people and communities as I have highlighted by the numerous examples in my book. It has been nearly 250 years since Thomas Jefferson wrote in the Declaration of Independence, "We hold these truths to be self-evident, that all men are created equal" and yet we are unfortunately still struggling to achieve that vision. The founding fathers knew the flaws of our country's origins, including the wretched sin of slavery, but nevertheless pressed ahead to create a republic that could be sustained and gradually advanced toward liberty for all. They knew that it would be a continuing struggle and that there would be many setbacks along the way. The death of civil rights leader John Lewis and release of the documentary of his life—*Good Trouble*—in 2020 reminds us that that the struggle for justice is long and goes well beyond one lifetime. I believe that the Presidential election of 2020 likely represented one of those transitional moments in American history which seem to come in each century. Whether we emerge from this transition stronger depends on our ability to rebuild our institutions and communities to serve the common good. This will be the work not of months, but of decades. It is not unlike the Civil Rights era of the twentieth century which is still a work in progress or early eras like the New Deal under President Franklin Roosevelt that lifted the country out of the Great Depression.

I close with a quote from the devotions of John Donne (1573–1631) and with another poem building on his theme. In "For Whom the Bell Tolls," Donne wrote,

> No man is an island, entire of itself; every man is a piece of the continent, a part of the main. If a clod be washed away by the sea, Europe is the less, as well as if a promontory were, as well as if a manor of thy friend's or of thine own were: any man's

death diminishes me, because I am involved in mankind, and therefore never send to know for whom the bells tolls; it tolls for thee.

Donne's perspective was given voice later in the well-known poem "First They Came for the Jews," attributed to Pastor Martin Niemöller:

First they came for the Jews
and I did not speak out
because I was not a Jew.

Then they came for the Communists
and I did not speak out
because I was not a Communist.

Then they came for the trade unionists
and I did not speak out
because I was not a trade unionist.

Then they came for me
and there was no one left to speak out for me.

Endnotes

1   Gary Maring, *Faith, Social Justice, and Public Policy*, 2012.

2   Gloria Guzman, *Median Household Income up in 2018 from 2017;* US Census Bureau, September 26, 2019.

3   *Out of Reach 2020;* National Low-Income Housing Coalition; Washington, DC.

4   Robert Jones, Public Religion Research Institute (PRRI), Washington, DC.

5   Mark Galli, Christianity Today, December 19, 2019.

6   Jeffrey M. Jones, *Presidential Moral Leadership Less Important to Republicans*, May 29, 2018.

7   Quinnipiac University National Poll, *He Does Not Provide Moral Leadership, Voters Say;* January 25, 2018.

8   Wikipedia, http://en.wikipedia.org/wiki/Dietrich_Bonhoeffer.

9   Goodreads, http://www.goodreads.com/author/quotes/29333.Dietrich_Bonhoeffer.

10 *Social Justice in the OECD—How Do the Member States Compare?*, http://www.bertelsmann-stiftung.de/bst/de/media/xcms_bst_dms_34886_34887_2.pdf.

11 Lutheran Volunteer Corp, at Luther Place Memorial Church in Washington, DC, http://www.lutheranvolunteercorps.org.

12 Steinbruck Center, Luther Place, Washington, DC, https://www.steinbruckcenter.org.

13 *Real Wage Trends, 1979 to 2018;* Congressional Research Service, updated July 23, 2019.

14 Oren Cass, *The Cost-of-Thriving Index—Reevaluating the Prosperity of the American Family*, Manhattan Institute, February 2020.

15 Lisa J. Dettling, Joanne W. Hsu, Lindsay Jacobs, Kevin B. Moore, and Jeffrey P. Thompson; *Recent Trends in Wealth-Holding by Race and Ethnicity: Evidence from the Survey of Consumer Finances*, Federal Reserve System; September 27, 2017.

16 *Federal Reserve Survey Report on the Economic Well-Being of U.S. Households in 2018*, Board of Governors of the Federal Reserve System, May 2019.

17 *COVID-19 Pandemic's Impact on Household Employment and Income;* Congressional Research Service, November 2020.

18   Best Countries 2019, *Global rankings, international news, and data insights*: U.S. News and World Report with BAV Group and Warton.

19   Kenneth Johnson and Daniel Lichter, *Rural Depopulation in a Rapidly Urbanizing America*, University of New Hampshire, Carsey School of Public Policy, February 6, 2019.

20   *Who Pays? A Distributional Analysis of the Tax Systems in All 50 States*, Economic Policy Institute, October 2018.

21   *The Long-Term Decline in Prime-Age Male Labor Force Participation*, Council of Economic Advisers, June 2016.

22   Angus Deaton and Anne Case, Princeton University, *Mortality and Morbidity in the 21st Century*, Brookings Institution, Brookings Papers on Economic Activity, Spring 2017.

23   S. R. Kegler, D. M. Stone, and K. M. Holland, *Trends in Suicide by Level of Urbanization—United States, 1999–2015. MMWR Morbidity and Mortality Weekly Report* 2017, 66:270–273, Centers for Disease Control and Prevention.

24   National Institutes of Health paper, *"Family Inequality: Diverging Patterns in Marriage, Cohabitation, and Childbearing,"* Journal of Economic Perspectives—Volume 30, Number 2—Spring 2016—Pages 79–102.

25   Edward N. Wolff, *Household Wealth Trends in the United States*, Working Paper 24085, November 2017.

26   Finance and Economics Discussion Series 2019-017, Divisions of Research & Statistics and Monetary Affairs, Federal Reserve Board.

27   *Wealth Inequality in the United States*; https://inequality.org/facts/wealth-inequality/

28   Rakesh Kochhar and Anthony Cilluffo; *How Wealth Inequality Has changed in the U.S. since the Great Recession, by Race, Ethnicity, and Income;* Pew Research Center, November 2017.

29   *Is the Middle Class within Reach for Middle-Income Families?* Governor Lael Brainard presented at Renewing the Promise of the Middle Class; 2019 Federal Reserve System Community Development Research Conference, Washington, DC; May 10, 2019.

30   Income and Poverty in the United States: 2018. Census Bureau Current Population Reports issued September 2019.

31   Emmanuel Saez, *Income and Wealth Inequality: Evidence and Policy Implications;* Berkeley, October 2016.

32   Business Review, Third Quarter 2015, Volume 98, Issue 3, Federal Reserve of Philadelphia.

33   OECD (2019); *OECD Employment Outlook 2019: The Future of Work;* OECD Publishing, Paris.

34   Congressional Budget Office, *The Distribution of Household Income, 2016;* July 2019.

35   OECD (2018), *OECD Employment Outlook 2018*, OECD Publishing, Paris.

36   *Who Pays? A Distributional Analysis of the Tax Systems in All 50 States*, Institute on Taxation and Economic Policy, October 2018.

37   Raj Chetty, David Grusky, Maximilian Hell, Nathaniel Hendre, Robert Manduca, and Jimmy Naran, *The Fading American Dream: Trends in Absolute Income Mobility Since 1940*, Working Paper 22910, National Bureau of Economic Research, December 2016.

38   Erik Brynjolfsson and Andrew McAfee, *The Second Machine Age: Work, Progress, and Prosperity in a Time of Brilliant Technologies--* of MIT, 2012.

39   McKinsey Global Institute, *Jobs Lost, Jobs Gained: Workforce Transitions in A Time of Automation*, December 2017.

40   http://www.vatican.va/holy_father/francesco/apost_exhortations/ documents/papa-francesco_esortazione-ap_20131124_evangelii-gaudium_en.html.

41   Michael J. Hicks and Srikant Devaraj, *The Myth and the Reality of American Manufacturing*, Ball State University, June 2015 and April 2017.

42   Lawrence H. Summers and Ed Balls, *Report of the Commission on Inclusive Prosperity*, Co-Chaired by, Convened by the Center for American Progress, January 2015.

43   *Wage Statistics for 2019, https://*www.ssa.gov/cgi-bin/netcomp.cgi?year=2019

44   *Income, Poverty and Health Insurance Coverage in the United States: 2019.* Bureau of the Census, Release Number CB20-145, September 2020.

45   United Nations study released in June 2018—"*Report of the Special Rapporteur on Extreme Poverty and Human Rights on His Mission to the United States of America.*"

46   Raj Chetty and Nathaniel Hendren, *The Effects of Neighborhoods on Intergenerational Mobility II: County-Level Estimates*, Harvard University, Equality of Opportunity Project.

47   Geoffrey Wodtke and David Harding of the University of Michigan and Felix Elwert of the University of Wisconsin, *Neighborhood Effects in Temporal Perspective: The Impact of Long-Term Exposure to Concentrated Disadvantage on High School Graduation.* American Sociological Review September 20, 2011 issue.

48   Robert Lee Wagmiller and Robert M. Adelman, Columbia: Academic Commons, 2009.

49   *The 2019 Annual Homeless Assessment Report (AHAR) to Congress*, US Dept. of Housing and Urban Development, January 2020.

50   Ta-Nehisi Coates, *Elegant Racism;* Atlantic Magazine, May 2014

51   *Looking Back to Move Forward: Progress and Lessons Learned During the First Four Years of Homeward DC,* September 2019, DC Government.

52 *Ahead of the Majority: Foregrounding Women of Color, An in-depth analysis of the women of color electorate in 2018*, AAPI and Groundswell Fund.

53 *Bipartisan Rx for America's Health Care: A Practical Path to Reform*; Bipartisan Policy Center, February 2020.

54 PRRI, *Emerging Consensus on LGBT Issues: Findings From the 2017 American Values Atlas*, May 2018.

55 *"Childhood Firearm Injuries in the United States"*: National Center for Injury Prevention and Control of the US Centers for Disease Control and Prevention (CDC).)

56 *Connecticut Handgun Licensing Law Associated with 40 Percent Drop in Gun Homicides, Johns* Hopkins Bloomberg School of Public Health, June 11, 2015.

57 *Fourth National Climate Assessment (NCA4) 2017/2018 in two volumes*, US Global Change Research Program.

58 A. Shepherd, E. Ivins, E. Rignot, et al. *Mass Balance of the Greenland Ice Sheet from 1992 to 2018*. Nature (2019).

59 *United Nations Global Environmental Outlook No. 6*, Cambridge Press, May 2019.

60 *Bipartisan Climate Roadmap*, by Climate Leadership Council, February 2020.

61 *The Sustainable Development Goals Report 2019*, United Nations, New York.

62 *The Costs of War project*, Brown University, Watson Institute, International and Public Affairs.

63 Internet Encyclopedia of Philosophy, http://www.iep.utm.edu/justwar//.

64 Joseph S Nye Jr., *Soft Power, The Means to Success in World Politics, Public Affairs, 2004*.

65 *Transforming Our World: The 2030 Agenda for Sustainable Development*, United Nations, 2015. sustainabledevelopment.un.org.

66 Irene Tung, Yannet Lathrop, and Paul Sonn, *The Growing Movement for $15*, November 2015, National Employment Law Project.